Discrimination on grounds of sexual orientation and gender identity in Europe

Council of Europe Publishing

The opinions expressed in this work are the responsibility of the author(s) and do not necessarily reflect the official policy of the Council of Europe.

All rights reserved. No part of this publication may be translated, reproduced or transmitted, in any form or by any means, electronic (CD-Rom, Internet, etc.) or mechanical, including photocopying, recording or any information storage or retrieval system, without prior permission in writing from the Public Information Division, Directorate of Communication (F-67075 Strasbourg Cedex or publishing@coe.int).

Cover design: Graphic Design Workshop, Council of Europe
Layout: Jouve, Paris

Council of Europe Publishing
F-67074 Strasbourg Cedex
http://book.coe.int

ISBN 978-92-871-6913-6
© Council of Europe, June 2011
Printed in France

Contents

Foreword 5

Summary 7

Recommendations 11

Introduction 17

1. Attitudes and perceptions 21

1.1. Lesbian, gay, bisexual and transgender persons 21

1.2. Criminalisation and medical classifications 22

1.3. Attitudes towards LGBT persons 25

1.4. Perceptions of the nation, religion and traditional values 29

1.5. Perceptions of LGBT persons' visibility and use of public space 31

1.6. Media 32

2. Legal standards and their implementation 35

2.1. Introduction 35

2.2. International and European standards 35

2.3. National standards 41

2.4. National structures for promoting equality 45

2.5. National policy initiatives 48

3. Protection: violence and asylum 51

3.1. Introduction 51

3.2. Violence against LGBT persons 52

3.3. Asylum on the grounds of sexual orientation and gender identity 62

4. Participation: freedoms of assembly, expression and association 71

4.1. Introduction 71

4.2. International and European standards 71

4.3. Situation in the member states 73

5. Privacy: gender recognition and family life 83

5.1. Introduction 83

5.2. Recognition of transgender persons' new gender and name 84

5.3. The right to marry and legally contract a partnership 91

5.4. Parenting and children 96

6. Access to health care, education and employment 103

6.1. Introduction 103

6.2. Health 103

6.3. Education 111

6.4. Employment 116

Conclusions 123

Appendix: Terms and concepts 129

Foreword

Many people in Europe are stigmatised because of their actual or perceived sexual orientation or gender identity and cannot fully enjoy their universal human rights. Some of them are victims of hate crime and may not receive protection when attacked in the street by fellow citizens, while some of their organisations are denied registration or are banned from organising peaceful meetings and demonstrations. Some people have fled to Council of Europe member states from countries where they risk being tortured or executed because of their sexual orientation or gender identity. Too few opinion leaders and leading politicians have taken a firm stand against homophobic and transphobic expressions, discrimination and violence.

I have often discussed these and other problems with the authorities of Council of Europe member states. The serious concerns about the problems faced by lesbian, gay, bisexual and transgender (LGBT) persons are reflected in my country monitoring reports as well as in thematic publications. I have also initiated a debate on the specific human rights issues encountered by transgender persons.

Unfortunately, I have repeatedly noted that there is too little objective data and information available to conduct a well-informed discussion with authorities on these questions. For this reason, my Office launched a comprehensive study on the situation concerning homophobia, transphobia and discrimination on grounds of sexual orientation and gender identity in the 47 member states of the Council of Europe. This report, coupled with a more comprehensive version, is the result of the study and contains a socio-legal analysis of the situation of LGBT persons across member states. The study relies on data and information made available by public authorities, national human rights structures, non-governmental organisations (NGOs) and academic experts in the member states.

I extend my gratitude to all organisations and people involved for their active participation and forthcoming contributions. Special thanks and recognition are due to the European Union Agency for Fundamental Rights (FRA), which kindly shared its research and data on the 27 member states of the European Union. In this regard, effective use was made of respective areas of expertise and complementary capacities.

The standards used in this report are based on judgments of the European Court of Human Rights and recent recommendations of the Council of Europe's Committee of Ministers and Parliamentary Assembly. Several institutions of the European Union, the Organization for Security and Co-operation in Europe (OSCE) and the United Nations have expressed concerns relating to the treatment of LGBT persons. The report clearly demonstrates that member states need to take further steps to address discrimination on grounds of sexual orientation and gender identity. It also provides a knowledge base for effective measures to combat homophobia and transphobia.

There is considerable resistance among many people to discuss the full enjoyment of universal human rights by LGBT persons. Even if this may not be a popular human rights topic, the time has now come to take the discussion forward and make it concrete. Supported by the facts presented in this report, I look forward to a constructive dialogue with authorities and other stakeholders to improve respect for the human rights of LGBT persons.

Thomas Hammarberg

Summary

This report is the result of the largest study ever made on homophobia, transphobia and discrimination on grounds of sexual orientation and gender identity in the 47 member states of the Council of Europe. The findings are presented in six thematic chapters followed by forward-looking conclusions. The Commissioner's recommendations on the issues that emerged from the findings of the study can be found at the beginning of the report.

Attitudes and perceptions

Homophobic and transphobic attitudes have been identified in all 47 member states, though attitudes vary significantly among and within the countries. Biased, outdated and incorrect information on what constitutes sexual orientation and gender identity as well as stereotypical portrayals of LGBT persons in the media and in textbooks contribute to the shaping of negative attitudes. Inflammatory and aggressive discourse against LGBT persons, occasionally amounting to hatred, has also been identified in several member states. LGBT persons have often been portrayed as a threat to the nation, religion, and traditional notions of gender and the family. Such speech has rarely been officially condemned.

The invisibility of LGBT persons and the absence of a serious discussion about their human rights situation are recurring themes in this report. Many LGBT individuals conceal their sexual orientation or gender identity in everyday life out of fear of negative reactions at school, work, in their neighbourhood or in their family. They fear that public knowledge of their sexual orientation and gender identity will lead to discrimination, harassment, rejection or even violence.

Legal standards and their implementation

A large number of member states have adopted legislative and other measures to prohibit discrimination against individuals on grounds of their sexual orientation and, though in fewer cases, also on grounds of gender identity. The majority of member states (38) have recognised, in line with international and European standards, that sexual orientation is one of the grounds of discrimination in comprehensive or sectoral non-discrimination legislation. Some nine member states do not appear to protect LGB persons against discrimination. A lower number, 20 out of 47 member states cover discrimination based on gender identity in their non-discrimination legislation, either as gender identity explicitly or as a recognised interpretation of the terms "sex", "gender" or "other ground of discrimination". For the other 27 member states, the non-discrimination legislation remains silent or is unclear on the protection of transgender persons.

Official statistics and data regarding discrimination on grounds of sexual orientation and gender identity are scarce in member states. National structures for promoting equality do not always have an explicit mandate to receive complaints of discrimination based on sexual orientation and even fewer have a clear mandate to cover gender identity as a ground of discrimination.

Protection: violence and asylum

LGBT persons run a serious risk of becoming victims of a hate crime or a hate-motivated incident, especially in public places. Violence may also take place within a family setting. Moreover, some state agents, such as the police, have been involved in blackmailing and harassing LGBT persons. Often LGBT persons do not report such violence to the competent authorities due to lack of trust in law-enforcement agencies, who may have no training in investigating effectively such hate-motivated crimes and incidents.

Homophobic and transphobic incidents or hate crimes are not reflected in official hate crime statistics in most of the member states. The incitement of hatred, violence or discrimination on grounds of sexual orientation is considered as a criminal offence in only 18 member states. Similarly, homophobic intent is accepted as an aggravating factor in common crimes in only 14 member states. In only two member states is gender identity or transphobic hate crime explicitly addressed in hate crime legislation.

Owing to criminalisation and persecution on grounds of sexual orientation and/or gender identity, a number of LGBT persons have sought to flee their country of origin. Thirty-three member states recognise sexual orientation as a ground for persecution in asylum claims, while only six member states do so for gender identity. LGBT persons encounter particular difficulties in the process of seeking asylum, often owing to inadequate knowledge by immigration authorities about conditions for LGBT persons in countries of origin. Some authorities appear to consider that, if LGBT persons kept their sexual orientation or gender identity secret, they would not be at risk. LGBT asylum seekers also face difficulties in asylum centres and may be exposed to harassment from other applicants.

Participation: freedoms of assembly, expression and association

Violent and discriminatory reactions have occurred when LGBT persons have collectively attempted to express their views, freely associate or gather for public demonstrations. In most member states the freedoms of association, expression and assembly of LGBT persons are respected. However, in a few states they have been infringed upon. Bans or administrative impediments imposed on public LGBT demonstrations were identified in 12 member states, and in some instances the police have failed to protect peaceful demonstrators from violent assaults. Obstructions and/or refusal of attempts to register LGBT associations have been identified in five member states, though in some instances courts have overturned such bans at a later stage. Infringement of the freedom of expression has been reported in three member states, whereas attempts to criminalise "propaganda of homosexuality" were identified in three member states.

Privacy: gender recognition and family life

Transgender persons face significant problems in the process of their legal gender recognition. In at least 10 member states no legislation regulating it was identified. In 13 other member states no or only partial legislation was identified, but transgender persons are able to have their new gender legally recognised, either through court decisions or by certain administrative practices. Twenty-nine member states require, as a precondition for legal gender recognition, surgery leading to infertility, whereas 15 member states require the transgender person to be unmarried or divorced, which can leave couples without a legally recognised relationship after divorce.

Same-sex couples wishing to marry can do so in seven member states (gender-neutral marriage) and in 13 other member states they can enter a registered partnership which provides a form of recognition. The lack of access to marriage or registered partnership deprives same-sex couples of rights and benefits granted to different-sex relationships. It has also consequences for same-sex couples having children as one of the partners may not have custody rights, inheritance and next-of-kin status, which need to be assured in the best interests of the child. Ten member states allow second-parent adoption to same-sex couples, while 35 countries provide no access to it. Two member states give only some parental authority and responsibilities to registered same-sex partnerships, but no adoption is available.

Access to health care, education and employment

LGBT persons are more prone to suffer from depression, anxiety, and anguish. Suicide and attempted suicide rates are significantly higher for LGBT persons than their heterosexual peers, especially young people. LGBT persons also experience problems when accessing health care, caused by mistrust between patients and doctors, problematic attitudes of medical staff, as well as outdated approaches to homosexuality and transgenderism. Contrary to international medical classifications, some official textbooks contain references to homosexuality as an illness. Transsexuality continues to be considered a mental disorder according to some international classifications. In 13 member states medical facilities for gender reassignment treatment are non-existent or insufficient. Health care insurance does not cover gender reassignment treatment in at least 16 countries. In the remaining states there is partial or full reimbursement.

Bullying of LGBT persons within the educational system is a reality. Objective information on sexual orientation and gender identity is rarely imparted in schools. Discrimination and harassment of LGBT persons also occurs in the employment sector. Even though the majority of member states include sexual orientation in non-discrimination legislation for employment, gender identity is usually only partially included under the sex or gender ground. Trade unions and employers in some member states have taken measures to combat these practices. Transgender persons face particular problems when accessing the labour market, as privacy of personally sensitive data related to their gender identity history is rarely ensured.

Recommendations

The Commissioner's recommendations build on the findings of this report and provide policy-oriented advice to member states to prevent and address homophobia, transphobia and discrimination on grounds of sexual orientation and gender identity.

The Commissioner for Human Rights recommends that authorities in Council of Europe member states should:

1. Attitudes and perceptions

1) Take a strong public position against violations of the human rights of LGBT persons and promote respect on issues related to sexual orientation and gender identity, for example through human rights education and awareness-raising campaigns.

2) Take steps to encourage factual, objective and professional reporting by the media on LGBT persons and issues related to sexual orientation and gender identity.

2. Legal standards and their implementation

1) Implement international human rights obligations without discrimination on grounds of sexual orientation and gender identity. The Yogyakarta Principles are a useful tool to provide guidance for implementing international human rights standards in relation to sexual orientation and gender identity. Member states are also encouraged to sign and ratify Protocol No. 12 to the European Convention on Human Rights on the general prohibition of discrimination.

2) Enact comprehensive national legislation on non-discrimination and include sexual orientation and gender identity among the prohibited grounds of discrimination. NGOs representing LGBT persons should be consulted and involved in the legislative process and in the preparation of policy measures for the implementation of the legislation.

3) Screen national legislation to detect and correct possible inconsistencies with non-discrimination legislation in force to prevent discrimination on grounds of sexual orientation and gender identity. Eliminate any discriminatory criminalisation of same-sex sexual activity if this is still present in the legislation.

4) Set up independent national structures for promoting equality and non-discrimination. The scope of their mandate should include discrimination on grounds of sexual orientation and gender identity.

5) Monitor the effectiveness of the implementation of national non-discrimination legislation and involve national human rights structures, including national structures for promoting equality, and organisations representing LGBT persons in the monitoring process. A regular monitoring mechanism should be put in place to this end.

3. Protection: violence and asylum

1) Include homophobic and transphobic hatred explicitly as possible motives in national legislation on bias-motivated crime and hate speech. Crimes targeting individuals or groups of people because of their perceived or real sexual orientation or gender identity should be punished and the bias motive taken into account as an aggravating circumstance.

2) Investigate effectively bias-motivated crimes, speech and incidents related to homophobia and transphobia. Specific training for law enforcement officials and members of the judiciary should be provided for this purpose.

3) Improve systematic data collection on hate-motivated crimes, speech and incidents related to homophobia and transphobia. Data on homophobic and transphobic crimes, speech, incidents and complaints should be clearly disaggregated from other hate-motivated crimes, speech and incidents.

4) Recognise that persecution or a well-founded fear of persecution on the basis of sexual orientation or gender identity may be valid grounds for granting refugee status and asylum. Unnecessarily invasive tests for LGBT asylum seekers for giving proof of their sexual orientation or gender identity should be avoided.

5) Provide expertise and training to asylum officers and other related professionals in order to ensure that LGBT asylum seekers are met in a respectful, informed and sensitive way during the asylum procedure. Procedures should be set up in a way that LGBT asylum seekers feel safe to disclose their sexual orientation or gender identity.

6) Address social isolation, violence and discrimination experienced by LGBT asylum seekers in asylum centres, and provide for their specific health care needs.

4. Participation: freedoms of assembly, expression and association

1) Respect the effective right to freedom of assembly of LGBT persons by ensuring that peaceful Pride festivals and other public events organised by LGBT people or focusing on issues related to sexual orientation and gender identity can take place without being subjected to discriminatory measures by the public authorities. Practices amounting to misuse of

legal or administrative provisions in order to hinder the organisation of such events should be prevented.

2) Provide effective protection to participants of peaceful Pride demonstrations or public events organised by and for LGBT persons from attacks and violent counter-demonstrations.

3) Respect the effective right to freedom of association of LGBT persons by ensuring, in particular, that non-governmental organisations representing LGBT persons or working on issues related to sexual orientation and gender identity can be set up and operate without being subjected to discriminatory measures by the public authorities. Administrative procedures which render the registration of these NGOs disproportionately lengthy or difficult should be prevented.

4) Respect the effective right to freedom of expression by safeguarding the possibility to receive and impart information on issues related to sexual orientation and gender identity in any form of expression such as the press, publications, oral and written statements, art and other media. Any discriminatory provision criminalising the dissemination and diffusion of factual information concerning sexual orientation and gender identity should be abolished. Unlawful interferences in the enjoyment of the right to freedom of expression by LGBT persons should be subject to criminal proceedings.

5. Privacy: gender recognition and family life

1) Grant legal recognition for the preferred gender of transgender persons and develop expeditious and transparent procedures for changing the name and sex of a transgender person on birth certificates, civil registers, identity cards, passports, educational certificates and other similar documents.

2) Abolish sterilisation and other compulsory medical treatment which may seriously impair the autonomy, health or well-being of the individual, as necessary requirements for the legal recognition of a transgender person's preferred gender.

3) Remove the requirement of being unmarried, or divorce for already married persons, as a necessary condition for the legal recognition of a transgender person's preferred gender.

4) Respect the right of transgender persons to effectively exercise their right to marry in accordance with their legally recognised gender.

5) Enact legislation recognising same-sex partnerships by granting such partnerships the same rights and benefits as different-sex partnerships or marriage, for example in the areas of social security, employment and pension benefits, freedom of movement, family reunification, parental rights and inheritance.

6) Grant same-sex couples and LGBT individuals, in compliance with the principle of the best interests of the child, similar opportunities as other applicants to be considered without discrimination as adoptive parents for a child.

7) Recognise the parental rights of same-sex parents, individually or jointly, including their rights of guardianship and custody without discrimination on grounds of their sexual orientation or gender identity. The parental rights of transgender persons should continue to be respected after the legal recognition of their preferred gender.

8) Allow access to assisted reproduction to LGBT persons without discrimination on grounds of their sexual orientation or gender identity.

9) Seek to provide adequate support for families with LGBT members in order to foster inclusion, respect and safety.

6. Access to health care, education and employment

1) Abolish outdated classification systems which portray homosexuality as an illness or disease.

2) Review any requirements of a diagnosis of mental disorder for accessing transgender health care in view of eliminating obstacles to the effective enjoyment, by transgender persons, of the rights to self-determination and the highest attainable standard of health.

3) Include in the education and training of health care professionals the importance of respecting the dignity of LGBT persons as well as their specific health care needs and choices.

4) Make gender reassignment procedures, such as hormone treatment, surgery and psychological support, accessible to transgender persons subject to informed consent and ensure that they are reimbursed by health insurance.

5) Promote respect and inclusion of LGBT persons at school and foster objective knowledge on issues concerning sexual orientation and gender identity in schools and other educational settings.

6) Combat bullying and harassment of LGBT students and staff. Schools should be a safe environment for LGBT students and staff, and teachers should be provided with tools to respond effectively to bullying and harassment of LGBT students.

7) Promote policies and practices aimed at combating discrimination based on sexual orientation or gender identity; also promote policies to foster diversity in the workplace together with initiatives which encourage the full inclusion and respect of LGBT staff in the work environment.

8) Respect the right of transgender persons to access the labour market by guaranteeing the respect of their privacy concerning the disclosure of personally sensitive data related to their gender identity and by promoting measures aimed at ending the exclusion and discrimination of transgender persons in the workplace.

7. Research and data collection

1) Encourage systematic research and disaggregated data collection concerning discrimination on grounds of sexual orientation and gender identity in all areas of life. LGBT-related questions should be included in general attitude surveys and public opinion polls.

2) Apply safeguards protecting the right to respect for private life of LGBT persons in the collection of any sensitive data.

Introduction

This report presents the results of the largest study ever made on homophobia, transphobia and discrimination on grounds of sexual orientation and gender identity in Europe.[1] It is published by the Commissioner for Human Rights of the Council of Europe and covers the 47 member states of the Council of Europe. The report is based on research and data collection primarily focused on the period 2004-2010 although some important data preceding this period have been included as well. Changes in policy and legislation in Council of Europe member states which took place after 31 December 2010 have not been systematically taken into account.

There have been two phases in the research and data-collection process. The first phase focused on the collection and comparative analysis of information and data of a legal nature (legislation and case law). This research was conducted through desk research and by national legal experts. The second phase focused on the collection and comparative analysis of data of a sociological nature. The aim of the sociological part of the study was to collect data on the everyday life of lesbian, gay, bisexual and transgender (LGBT) persons in the 47 member states. This part of the research was conducted by desk research and field visits in the member states. The research and data-collection process was co-ordinated by the international consultancy firm COWI.

During the field visits, semi-structured qualitative interviews were conducted with key stakeholders in each member state.[2] The relevant stakeholders provided oral statements as well as written materials, which gave a broad overview of the issues at stake. To start with, representatives of national authorities, in most instances officials working in the Ministry of Justice, Ministry of the Interior, Ministry of Foreign Affairs or Ministry of Health were met in order to access available official data and statistics. This could include information regarding discrimination on grounds of sexual orientation and gender identity and incidents of homophobia and transphobia as well as information on the relevant national policies, action plans, and "good practice" related to combating discrimination and promoting human rights. These interviews aimed to collect information but also to gauge awareness of the national situation with regard to homophobia, transphobia and discrimination among the interlocutors. Many interlocutors emphasised the usefulness of this study and engaged constructively in the data-collection process, though on many occasions there were not many statistics or data to share. Public authorities have generally been co-operative in their contribution to the study.

---

1. Voluntary contributions for this project were provided by Belgium (Flemish Government), Finland, Germany, the Netherlands, Norway, the Swedish International Development Cooperation Agency (SIDA), Switzerland and the United Kingdom.
2. With the exception of Andorra, where no field visit took place (phone interviews were conducted instead). Furthermore, meetings with the Russian authorities during the field visit in the Russian Federation did not take place. In the national contributions (sociological reports) a precise overview per country is given regarding the interlocutors interviewed.

Organisations representing LGBT persons were also met, usually LGBT organisations as well as human rights non-governmental organisations. Representatives of LGBT organisations provided their perspectives on the information collected and directed attention to further materials. LGBT organisations, having hands-on experience and knowledge of various aspects of the situation for LGBT persons, have been a valuable source of data. This is particularly the case when research and/or official data have been scarce. The European Region of the International Lesbian, Gay, Bisexual, Trans and Intersex Association (ILGA-Europe) and Transgender Europe (TGEU) provided additional information. In addition, consultations regarding the research design and implementation took place at regular intervals with ILGA-Europe and Transgender Europe.

Furthermore, representatives of national human rights structures (that is, national human rights institutions, ombudsman institutions and equality bodies) were met during the field trips. Whereas this report shows that not all these structures are currently engaged in combating discrimination based on sexual orientation and gender identity, the meetings turned out to be useful. Once again, on most occasions, representatives of these national structures emphasised the need for more engagement in this area.

Based on the information and data collected for each country, a legal and a sociological report were drafted for each Council of Europe member state. Regarding the 27 member states of the European Union, this report draws primarily from research conducted by the European Union Agency for Fundamental Rights (FRA). Relevant FRA publications from 2008, 2009 and 2010[3] as well as data from primary research as published in the FRA's national contributions (reports on the social situation and – updated – legal reports) were key resource documents. In line with the co-operation agreement between the FRA and the Council of Europe,[4] these reports and data were shared by the FRA with the Office of the Commissioner for Human Rights. The Commissioner's Office was also able to benefit from the technical expertise of the FRA throughout the research process.

As regards the other 20 member states of the Council of Europe, the legal and sociological reports were drafted by consultants and national experts. All reports have been quality assured by independent reviewers. However, any views or opinions expressed in the national country reports do not necessarily represent those of the Office of the Commissioner for Human Rights. These two sets of 47 national reports form the basis for the comparative report. For readability of this summary report, footnote referencing has been limited

---

3. See European Union Agency for Fundamental Rights, "Homophobia and Discrimination on the grounds of Sexual Orientation and Gender Identity in the European Union Member States: Part 1 – Legal Analysis", 2008; "Homophobia and Discrimination on Grounds of Sexual Orientation and Gender Identity in the European Union Member States: Part II – The Social Situation", 2009; "Homophobia, Transphobia and Discrimination on Grounds of Sexual Orientation and Gender Identity: 2010 Update – Comparative Legal Analysis", 2010.
4. Agreement between the European Community and the Council of Europe on cooperation between the European Union Agency for Fundamental Rights and the Council of Europe, paragraph 7.

to the most necessary information. Full details and references can be found in the comprehensive version of the report and the national reports, which will be made available separately. Information provided by the Organization for Security and Co-operation in Europe (OSCE) Office for Democratic Institutions and Human Rights (ODIHR) and the Office of the United Nations High Commissioner for Refugees (UNHCR) was also used in the compilation of this report.

It should be pointed out that research for this report was conducted in areas which face serious challenges regarding data availability. Systematically collected data on homophobia, transphobia and discrimination on grounds of sexual orientation and gender identity in most member states remain scarce or simply non-existent. The lack of data requires serious scrutiny, a conclusion backed by the fact that many of the public authorities met during field visits expressed the need for improving the collection and handling of data. Significant improvements in data collection would be needed in order to acquire comprehensive data sets on the socio-legal position of LGBT persons.

The report is structured in the following manner.

The Commissioner's recommendations to member states, which build on the findings of the report, can be found at the beginning of the volume.

The report starts with a chapter providing a general overview of attitudes and perceptions towards LGBT persons. Attitudinal surveys, research and studies related to Council of Europe member states are presented here. This overview can be considered as a general contextual introduction for the thematic chapters to follow.

Chapter 2 outlines the applicable international and European human rights standards from the perspective of non-discrimination followed by a summary of the relevant national legal frameworks with reference to sexual orientation and gender identity as prohibited grounds for discrimination. This chapter also looks into national implementation of non-discrimination legislation, including the work conducted by national structures for promoting equality and policy initiatives undertaken by member states.

Chapter 3 focuses on the right to life and security as protected by international human rights law. It demonstrates the extent to which LGBT persons are victims of hate crimes, hate speech and other violent acts. In addition, this chapter explores the protection mechanisms in place for asylum seekers who have fled countries where they face persecution due to their sexual orientation or gender identity.

Chapter 4 covers the participation of LGBT persons in society through their full enjoyment of the freedoms of association, expression and assembly. In this chapter, obstacles related to the organisation of Pride events as well as problems of registering LGBT organisations are discussed.

Chapter 5 considers aspects of private and family life. It highlights the specific problems transgender persons encounter in obtaining legal recognition of their preferred gender. The recognition of same-sex partnerships and parental rights with reference to the best interests of the child are also discussed in this chapter.

Chapter 6 discusses the access of LGBT persons to health care, education and employment. This chapter analyses the extent to which LGBT persons enjoy their rights to the highest attainable standard of health, education and employment which are essential for their social inclusion and well-being.

General conclusions can be found at the end of the report. They are policy-oriented and forward-looking. The terms and concepts used in the report are explained in an Appendix.

1. Attitudes and perceptions

1.1. Lesbian, gay, bisexual and transgender persons

Lesbian, gay, bisexual and transgender (LGBT) persons are present in all Council of Europe member states. This heterogeneous group of persons is often stigmatised and faces homophobia, transphobia, discrimination and the fear of being rejected by family, relatives, friends and society at large due to their sexual orientation or gender identity. For this reason, LGBT persons may not be able to share this most intimate aspect of their private life with family, friends and colleagues.

While the "LGBT" label has been used as a self-designatory cluster to denote the group concerned in political and human rights discourse, in this report this collective designation is merely used as an umbrella term. It is important to note that many people considered as LGBT may individually not feel the need to identify themselves under this designation. Other people, including intersex persons or those who identify themselves as "queer", may associate themselves with the LGBT community, which can then be collectively referred to as "LGBTIQ". Yet others may point out that the human rights issues affecting lesbian, gay, bisexual and transgender persons respectively are significantly different for each sub-group concerned, despite the interconnected nature of the encountered discrimination, and would therefore require different approaches.

In the 1940s lesbian and gay persons in Europe began to meet collectively and set up groups and organisations representing them, sometimes at a time when homosexuality was still a criminal offence. The oldest still-existing organisations in Council of Europe member states were founded in 1946 (the Netherlands) and 1948 (Denmark). In the following decades, such groups and organisations were gradually established in many member states in Western Europe along with other social movements throughout the 1960s and 1970s. They also gradually started to address the demands of bisexual persons. The consolidation of many lesbian and gay organisations in Central and Eastern Europe followed after the political changes of the 1990s in that region. The International Lesbian and Gay Association (ILGA) was founded in 1978 and its European regional section (ILGA-Europe) representing lesbian, gay, bisexual, transgender and intersex persons was set up in 1996.

Groups and organisations representing transgender persons were set up at a later stage, with some of them founded in the 1990s and others in the new millennium. Transgender Europe (TGEU), an organisation building a European network of transgender groups and activists, has existed since 2005. In recent years, political advocacy on transgender human rights and community building of transgender persons have strengthened considerably, due to the consolidation of TGEU and other transgender groups, and because several LGB organisations have gradually started to address the human rights of transgender persons as well.

1.2. Criminalisation and medical classifications

The Committee of Ministers of the Council of Europe stated in 2010 that "lesbian, gay, bisexual and transgender persons have been for centuries and are still subjected to homophobia, transphobia and other forms of intolerance and discrimination even within their family – including criminalisation, marginalisation, social exclusion and violence – on grounds of sexual orientation or gender identity".[5] It should thus not come as a surprise that for a long time LGBT persons in many Council of Europe member states remained – and in some member states still are – invisible. Only in the second half of the last century – and with notable differences between the 47 countries – have LGBT persons and their organisations become more visible in society and participatory in human rights debates.

Two historical circumstances, one of a legal and the other of a medical nature, offer partial explanations for the invisibility of LGBT persons in society and the absence of sexual orientation and gender identity in relevant political and human rights debates. First, different forms of criminalisation of same-sex consensual sexual acts between adults – primarily between men, as women were often not considered in this context – have been found for shorter or longer periods in the criminal codes or legal traditions of nearly all Council of Europe member states.[6] The first countries to decriminalise such acts did so in the 18th century while the last countries only did so at the beginning of the 21st century (see Table 1.1).[7] Accession criteria to become a member state of the Council of Europe played a part in the process. In countries where homosexuality was criminalised it was often impossible to be openly p. 23 gay or lesbian and to set up and register organisations advocating for the rights of this community.

No Council of Europe member state criminalises same-sex sexual acts as such any longer, even though there are still provisions in the criminal law of some Council of Europe member states which explicitly discriminate on the basis of

---

5. Committee of Ministers Recommendation CM/Rec(2010)5 on measures to combat discrimination on grounds of sexual orientation or gender identity, adopted on 31 March 2010, preamble.
6. Waaldijk C., "Civil Developments: Patterns of Reform in the Legal Position of Same-sex Partners in Europe", *Canadian Journal of Family Law*, 17(1) (2000), pp. 62-64. See also Foucault M., *The history of sexuality*, vol. 1 (An Introduction), 1976.
7. This table is based on the following sources: Leroy-Forgeot F., *Histoire juridique de l'homosexualité en Europe*, Paris: Presses Universitaires de France 1997; Graupner H., "Sexual Consent: The Criminal Law in Europe and Outside of Europe", in H. Graupner and V. L. Bullough (eds), *Adolescence, Sexuality and the Criminal Law*, Haworth Press, New York, 2005, pp. 111-171; Waaldijk K., "Legal recognition of homosexual orientation in the countries of the world", paper for the conference "The Global Arc of Justice – Sexual Orientation Law around the World" (Los Angeles, 11-14 March 2009); Ottosson, D., *State-sponsored Homophobia*, ILGA, Brussels, 2010. These sources contradict each other on some points, partly because the enactment of a law and its entry into force do not always take place in the same year. In some member states decriminalisation took part in different years in different parts of the country, and in a few other states different penal provisions were repealed in different years. Please note that national borders have changed over time and that some of the member states listed here can be considered as successors to earlier states existing in the corresponding geographical area. According to the Andorran authorities, same-sex consensual acts have never been criminalised in the country.

sexual orientation.[8] The legacy of criminalisation and the fairly recent removal of criminalisation provisions in some member states have contributed to the stigma historically attached to homosexuality and attitudes towards LGBT persons which are, as this report will show, still negative in many regards. In fact, surveys demonstrate that in some member states the majority of the population may still believe that homosexuality is illegal. The United Nations Special Rapporteur on the Right of Everyone to the Enjoyment of the Highest Attainable Standard of Physical and Mental Health has stated that "criminalization may not be the sole reason behind stigma, but it certainly perpetuates it, through the reinforcement of existing prejudices and stereotypes".[9]

The second historical factor lies in the medical field. LGBT persons were, and many still are, regarded as being ill or suffering from a disease. Only in 1990 did the World Health Organization (WHO) remove homosexuality from the *International Statistical Classification of Diseases and Related Health Problems* (ICD).[10] The American Psychiatric Association removed homosexuality (which was defined as a mental disorder) from the *Diagnostic and Statistical Manual of Mental Disorders* (DSM) in 1973.[11] Despite the removal of homosexuality from the list of diseases, this report has found evidence that in some member states of the Council of Europe health practitioners, official health policies and some textbooks in schools still apply these outdated classifications leading to factually incorrect information on homosexuality. This is compounded by the fact that public opinion in many member states considers homosexuality as a biological disorder or an illness that needs to be cured.

In a similar manner, systems for classifying mental disorders have a direct impact on the way transgender persons are perceived by society. The WHO lists transsexualism as a mental and behavioural disorder in the ICD.[12] Transgender persons are thus labelled as having a psychiatric pathologisation. The American Psychiatric Association[13] includes the term "gender identity disorder" as a mental health disorder in its DSM and uses it to describe persons who experience significant gender dysphoria, that is, discontent with the biological sex they are born with. This report has identified serious obstacles for many transgender persons in accessing basic services, particularly health services, due to these classification systems and, more widely, in accessing their right to be legally recognised in their preferred gender.

---

8. For example, in Gibraltar (United Kingdom) an unequal age of consent for homosexual and heterosexual relationships is still applied. The issue has been brought to the attention of the Gibraltar Supreme Court. Article 347 of the Greek Penal Code incriminates contact "against nature" between males in certain situations.
9. Human Rights Council, "Report of the Special Rapporteur on the Right of Everyone to the Enjoyment of the Highest Attainable Standard of Physical and Mental Health, Anand Grover", A/HRC/14/20, paragraph 22, 27 April 2010.
10. World Health Organization, *International Statistical Classification of Diseases and Related Health Problems*, 1990.
11. American Psychiatric Association, *Diagnostic and Statistical Manual of Mental Disorders* (4th edn), 1994.
12. World Health Organization, *International Statistical Classification of Diseases and Related Health Problems*, Tenth Revision, Version for 2007.
13. American Psychiatric Association, *Diagnostic and Statistical Manual of Mental Disorders*, Washington, DC (4th edn), 2000.

Table 1.1: Decriminalisation of same-sex consensual acts between adults

Country	Year of decriminalisation
Armenia	2003
Azerbaijan	2001
Georgia	2000
Cyprus	1998
Bosnia and Herzegovina	1998 [BiH] / 2000 [Rep. Srp.] 2001 [Brcko District]
"the former Yugoslav Republic of Macedonia"	1996
Romania	1996
Albania	1995
Moldova	1995
Serbia	1994
Ireland	1993
Lithuania	1993
Russian Federation	1993
Estonia	1992
Latvia	1992
Ukraine	1991
Liechtenstein	1989
Portugal	1945 / 1983
The United Kingdom	1967 [England+Wales] / 1981 [Scotland] / 1982 [Northern Ireland]
Spain	1822 / 1979
Croatia	1977
Montenegro	1977
Slovenia	1977
Malta	1973
Norway	1972
Austria	1971
Finland	1971
Germany	1968 [DDR] / 1969 [BRD]
Bulgaria	1968
Hungary	1962
Czech Republic	1962
Slovak Republic	1962
Greece	1951
Sweden	1944
Switzerland	1942
Iceland	1940
Denmark	1933
Poland	1932
Italy	1810 / 1890
San Marino	1865
Turkey	1858
The Netherlands	1811
Belgium	1794
Luxembourg	1794
Monaco	1793
France	1791
Andorra	–

The legacy of criminalisation and medical classifications naturally do not account for a full explanation for the longstanding invisibility of LGBT persons and the lack of discussion on sexual orientation and gender identity discrimination. Other factors, discussed below, have also played a major role. Yet the criminalising and medical discourses have directly influenced perceptions on the states' human rights obligations to address the discrimination of LGBT persons and combat homophobia and transphobia.

1.3. Attitudes towards LGBT persons

Attitudes towards LGBT persons are not homogeneous across Europe or within the member states. They range from very negative to very positive. Their articulation may vary depending on a specific subject matter (access to marriage for same-sex couples) or political context (at election time defending the human rights of LGBT persons may not be considered attractive by some politicians). European and national public opinion surveys and research have measured the attitudes of the general population towards LGBT persons. These European studies include the Eurobarometer[14] as well as the European Values Study[15] and the European Social Survey.[16] Such studies have focused on questions related to whether gay men and lesbian women should be free to live their life as they wish, how people feel about having a gay or lesbian neighbour or whether a gay or lesbian person should hold the highest political office in the country.

European studies

Some differences between European attitude studies exist relating to the geographical focus: not all surveys include all Council of Europe member states. Secondly, the use of different methodologies is common: normally the focus is on lesbian and gay persons only rather than on bisexual and transgender persons. This often makes the figures incomparable. However, some overall patterns can be identified in these studies. For example, regarding opinions on the statement: "Gay men and lesbians should be free to live their own life as they wish", respondents in Sweden, the Netherlands and Denmark register the lowest levels of disagreement with the statement (about 10% of respondents disagreeing).[17] In the same survey, respondents in Ukraine, Romania, Turkey and the Russian Federation give the highest rates of disagreement (about 70% of respondents disagreeing with the statement).

---

14. European Commission, Special Eurobarometer 296, "Discrimination in the European Union: Perceptions, Experiences and Attitudes", 2008; European Commission, Special Eurobarometer 317, "Discrimination in the EU", 2009.
15. European Values Study, "How do Europeans think about life, family, work, religion, sex, politics, and society?".
16. European Social Survey, "Exploring Public Attitudes, Informing Public Policy. Selected Findings from the First Three Rounds", 2005.
17. European Social Survey, "Exploring Public Attitudes, Informing Public Policy. Selected Findings from the First Three Rounds", 2005, pp. 16-17.

Regarding opinions on the question "How would you personally feel about having a homosexual as a neighbour?" a 2008 report concluded that for the European Union member states "the average European is largely comfortable with the idea of having a homosexual person as a neighbour".[18] However, there are large differences between countries, with respondents in Sweden (9.5), the Netherlands and Denmark (9.3) being the most comfortable with this idea (see Map 1.1) on a 10-point "comfort scale". Respondents in Romania (4.8), Bulgaria (5.3), Latvia (5.5) and Lithuania (6.1) are less comfortable. Other studies measuring attitudes and "social distance" found similar patterns.[19]

Map 1.1: "How would you personally feel about having a homosexual as a neighbour?"[20]

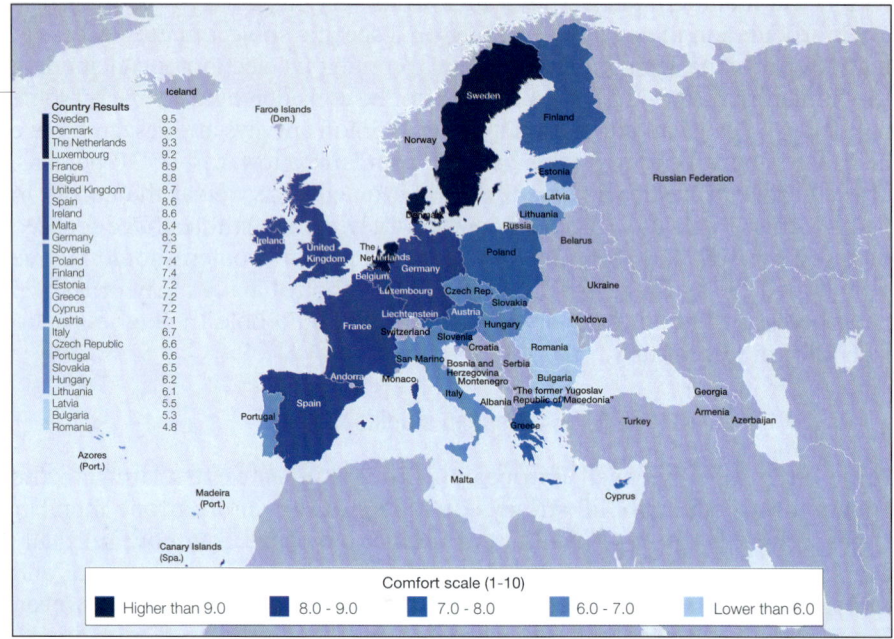

As for the question whether a homosexual person should hold the highest political office in the country, it was found in 2008 that people in Sweden, Denmark and the Netherlands were the most positive while people in Bulgaria, Cyprus and Romania were the most negative.[21] The question was repeated in 2009 and the most negative answers were found in Bulgaria, Romania and Turkey.[22]

---

18. European Commission, Special Eurobarometer 296, "Discrimination in the European Union: Perceptions, Experiences and Attitudes", 2008, p. 57.
19. European Commission, Special Eurobarometer 317, "Discrimination in the EU", 2009; European Values Survey 1999/2000, pp. 85-91.
20. All maps in this report are for illustrative purposes only to indicate the countries covered by the report.
21. European Commission, Special Eurobarometer 296, "Discrimination in the European Union: Perceptions, Experiences and Attitudes", 2008, p. 58.
22. European Commission, Special Eurobarometer 317, "Discrimination in the EU", 2009, p. 91.

Analysing the socio-demographic and political profile of the respondents, the Eurobarometer found that men are usually more negative than women, older generations more negative than young, less-educated persons more negative than higher-educated, and persons with right-wing political views more negative than those with left-wing political views. A crucial factor contributing to more positive attitudes towards LGBT persons is to have them as friends or acquaintances. The Eurobarometer survey from 2008 shows a correlation between those respondents who have homosexual acquaintances themselves and a positive attitude towards having a homosexual person as a neighbour, or as a country leader.[23] The lowest proportion of people who state that they have homosexual acquaintances are found in Romania (3%), Latvia (6%) and Bulgaria (7%), whereas the highest proportion of people with homosexual acquaintances are found in the Netherlands (69%), Sweden (56%), Denmark, France and the United Kingdom (all 55%).

As the Eurobarometer concludes:

> It is quite stunning how potent an influence diversity in one's social circle is upon attitudes to minorities. Being open-minded and having contact with minorities is the factor with the most positive influence on people's attitudes. When rating out of 10 how comfortable (with 10 being completely comfortable) they would feel with an LGBT person attaining the highest elected office in the land, those with LGBT friends gave an average rating of 8.5, while those without gave an average rating of 5.5 – a significantly lower rating. This sort of finding is now consistent across three waves of this Eurobarometer study and is, no doubt, going to continue being so.[24]

This was also recognised by an expert in the Russian Federation: "Very few people in Russia have personal acquaintances with lesbian, gay or bisexual persons. Even fewer people know transgender persons, because it is a very new phenomenon in our society. People with personal relations with LGBT have a higher degree of tolerance."[25]

National surveys in Council of Europe member states

In many Council of Europe member states similar surveys have been conducted, again with different methodologies, focus and scope. Regarding survey results related to having a gay or lesbian neighbour, a Turkish survey from 2009[26] showed that 87% of the population did not want to have a gay or lesbian neighbour – the same figure is found in an Armenian survey from 2005.[27] A survey from Croatia in 2002 indicated that a little less than half of the people surveyed would not like a gay or lesbian person as a neighbour.[28]

---

23. European Commission, Special Eurobarometer 296, "Discrimination in the European Union: Perceptions, Experiences and Attitudes", 2008, Chapter 9, p. 53.
24. European Commission, Special Eurobarometer 317, "Discrimination in the EU", 2009, p. 119.
25. National contribution (sociological report) on the Russian Federation, p. 7.
26. Esmer Y., "Radicalism and Extremism", Bahcesehir University, 2009.
27. Carroll A. and Quinn S., "Forced out: LGBT people in Armenia", ILGA-Europe/COC Netherlands, 2007, p. 34.
28. National contribution (sociological report) on Croatia, p. 5.

In 2007, in a survey held in "the former Yugoslav Republic of Macedonia", 62% of those surveyed answered that it is "unacceptable to have neighbours who have sexual relations with people from the same sex". [29]

It should be kept in mind that the "neighbour" question is just one indicator of attitudes. Similar questions have been asked in relation to other contexts such as the workplace, education and personal acquaintances and friendships. A study in Cyprus, for example, found that respondents would be more uncomfortable with gay or lesbian persons teaching their child than if the person was a colleague or a neighbour.[30] In a study from Bosnia and Herzegovina, 71% of respondents believed that they would feel very uncomfortable in the company of a gay or lesbian person. Some 82% held negative opinions about gays and lesbians, although it is worth noting that the focus of the study was to register public opinions on homosexuality and prostitution.[31] According to a Lithuanian study,[32] 62% would not like to belong to any organisation with gay and lesbian members, 69% did not want gay or lesbian persons to work in schools and 50% objected to gay or lesbian persons working in the police force.

In Georgia 84% of respondents expressed negative attitudes towards homosexuality.[33] Significantly more positive figures are found in a survey from the Netherlands, according to which "the percentage of the population who can be characterised as 'anti-gay' fell from 15% in 2006 to 9% in 2009".[34]

Surveys related to transgender persons are rare. In only two member states did studies focus on attitudes towards transgender persons. A study in the United Kingdom concluded that discriminatory attitudes are particularly common in respect of transgender persons.[35] A study in Germany found that 45% agreed to the statement that they have no or little understanding of those who intend to or have changed their gender.[36]

---

29. Coalition for Protection and Promotion of Sexual and Health Rights of Marginalised Communities, "Annual Report on sexual and health rights of marginalised communities", 2009, p. 41.
30. Cyprus College Research Center, "Attitudes and Perceptions of the Public towards Homosexuality", 2006.
31. Prism Research, "Researching Public Opinion about Homosexuality and Prostitution", Sarajevo, 2005, cited in Durkovic S., "The Invisible Q?: Human Rights Issues and Concerns of LGBTIQ Persons in Bosnia and Herzegovina", p. 19.
32. The Market and Opinion Research Centre Vilmorus Ltd, "Discrimination against Various Social Groups in Lithuania", 2006, also quoted in: European Union Agency for Fundamental Human Rights, "Homophobia and Discrimination on Grounds of Sexual Orientation and Gender Identity in the European Union Member States: Part II – The Social Situation", 2009, p. 34.
33. Quinn S., "Forced Out: LGBT People in Georgia", ILGA-Europe/COC Netherlands, 2007, p. 26.
34. Keuzenkamp S., "Steeds gewoner, nooit gewoon. Acceptatie van homoseksualiteit in Nederland", Sociaal en Cultureel Planbureau, The Hague, 2010.
35. Bromley C., Curtice J. and Given L., "Attitudes to discrimination in Scotland: 2006, Scottish Social Attitudes Survey", Scottish Government Social Research, Edinburgh, 2007, p. ix.
36. Federal Anti-Discrimination Agency, Benachteiligung von Trans Personen, insbesondere im Arbeitsleben, Berlin, 2010, p. 62.

1.4. Perceptions of the nation, religion and traditional values

Despite differences between member states in their populations' attitudes towards LGBT persons, there are similarities across member states as regards the perceptions underpinning such attitudes. The first set of perceptions relates to the nation, religion and traditional values on gender roles, sexuality and the family.

In some member states, being gay or lesbian is viewed as a "betrayal" of national values and unity. Such arguments may be grounded on a specific understanding of the nation or the state which aims to preserve the homogeneity of the nation. For example, an interlocutor from the authorities explained that in Armenia being homosexual is often seen as disloyal to the traditional values of the Armenian people.[37] In other countries, LGBT persons may also be seen as damaging the unity and moral order of the country. With reference to the organisation of an LGBT Pride parade in the Russian Federation, the Moscow Patriarchate was quoted as stating that it "infringes on our multi-ethnic nation's moral norms, on public order, and in the long run – on people's future. … If people refuse to procreate, the nation degrades. So the gay propaganda ultimately aims at ruining our nation."[38] In a study from Bosnia and Herzegovina 77% of respondents believed that accepting homosexuality would be detrimental for the country.[39] In a Serbian study, half of the respondents thought that homosexuality was dangerous to society, and that state institutions should work to prevent homosexuality.[40]

In other member states certain political groups use the "national values" argument in the promotion of respect for LGBT persons as a marker of tolerance inherent in their national culture. They stress that their national culture is fundamentally different from the national cultures of immigrant communities. For example, in Denmark, Germany and the Netherlands attitudes of immigrant and in particular Muslim communities are portrayed by some political groups as anti-western.[41] This has generated debates on what is termed "homo-nationalism" as pointed out by Judith Butler: "We all have noticed that gay, bisexual, lesbian, trans and queer people can be instrumentalised by those who want to wage wars, i.e. cultural wars against migrants by means of

---

37. National contribution (sociological report) on Armenia, p. 5.
38. Moscow Patriarchate Department of External Church Relations, quoted by Interfax, "Stop gay propaganda in Russia – Moscow Patriarchate", 23 May 2007.
39. Prism Research, "Researching Public Opinion about Homosexuality and Prostitution", Sarajevo, 2005, cited in Durkovic S., "The Invisible Q?: Human Rights Issues and Concerns of LGBTIQ Persons in Bosnia and Herzegovina", p. 19.
40. Gay Straight Alliance, "Prejudices Exposed – Homophobia in Serbia". Public opinion research report on LGBT population, 2008, research conducted for Gay Straight Alliance by Centre for Free Elections and Democracy (CeSID), February-March 2008, p. 5.
41. Drud-Jensen M. T. and Knudsen S. P., "Ondt i røven. Folk der har ondt i røven over bøsser – bøsser der har ondt i røven over folk", Copenhagen: Høst & Søn, 2005; Simon B. (2007) *Einstellungen zur Homosexualität: Ausprägungen und sozialpsychologische Korrelate bei Jugendlichen mit und ohne Migrationshintergrund*, Christian-Albrechts-Universität, Kiel; Mepschen P. "Sex and the Other – Homosexuality and Islam in Dutch public discourse", University of Amsterdam (Master's thesis), 2008.

forced islamophobia. ... Currently, many European governments claim that our gay, lesbian, queer rights must be protected and we are made to believe that the new hatred of immigrants is necessary to protect us."[42] Ideas of the nation can thus be used to embrace LGBT persons or be used to dissociate them from others, be it the national majority or immigrant populations.

Second, negative attitudes towards LGBT persons are also shaped by religious beliefs, such as that LGBT persons are sinful and acting against religious teaching. Such arguments draw upon a particular interpretation of religion to support the view that LGBT persons are detrimental to religion or religious believers. This report found many examples of such statements by influential religious leaders, as well as opinion leaders. In 2010, before a debate in the Parliamentary Assembly of the Council of Europe on a report focusing on LGBT human rights, different religious communities in Georgia collaboratively protested about "abnormalities, such as homosexuality, bisexuality and other sexual perversions, that are considered not only by Christianity but also by all other traditional religions as the greatest sin, causing degeneration and physical and mental illnesses".[43] However, while many religious leaders brand homosexuality as immoral and issue warnings of a demographic threat, others, like Archbishop Desmund Tutu, have highlighted that combating discrimination against LGBT persons is a matter of ordinary justice: "We struggled against apartheid in South Africa because we were being blamed and made to suffer for something we could do nothing about. It is the same with homosexuality."[44]

Third, traditional values can relate to notions of gender and the family: LGBT persons are then seen as transgressing the normative perceptions and boundaries of what it entails to be a "man" or a "woman". This is considered to be provocative and unacceptable. Various stakeholders from, among others, Albania, Italy, Georgia, Greece, Montenegro and Ukraine pointed out that in their societies patriarchal values, including concepts about masculinity and femininity, were strong.[45] Transgender persons are particularly affected by such values, in the sense that transgender persons are not always identifiable as either male or female. They face negative attitudes, ridicule and outright rejection in public. Traditional notions of gender can also relate to the concept of the family in the sense that LGBT persons are perceived as a threat to heterosexual families.

---

42. Butler J., "I must Distance Myself From This Complicity with Racism", Civil Courage Refusal Speech, Christopher Street Day, Berlin, 19 June 2010. Speech made by the author when she refused to accept a Civil Courage Prize.
43. Joint written statement by the Patriarch of the Georgian Orthodox Church, the Ambassador Extraordinary and Plenipotentiary of the Holy See to Georgia, Head of the Georgian Eparchy of the Armenian Apostle Church, Acting Chief Rabbi of Georgia and the Plenipotentiary Representative of the Caucasian Muslims' Organisation in Georgia, 29 January 2010.
44. Baird V., Tutu D. and Perry G., *Sex, Love and Homophobia*, Amnesty International, 2004.
45. National contribution (sociological report) on Georgia, p. 5; National contribution (sociological report) on Montenegro, p. 5; "Ukrainian Homosexuals and Society: A Reciprocation – Review of the situation: society, authorities and politicians, mass-media, legal issues, gay-community", Kiev, 2007, p. 67.

1.5. Perceptions of LGBT persons' visibility and use of public space

Another set of perceptions relate to notions of what constitutes the private and the public space. Acts perceived as uneventful and unassuming for heterosexual couples (for example, holding hands, kissing or talking about their private life) may often be perceived as provocative and offensive when done by LGBT persons. Some representatives of national human rights structures in member states lent a degree of understanding to such attitudes by expressing views that there should not necessarily be public venues, such as clubs and bars, for LGBT persons, or that resistance against public LGBT manifestations was understandable because they were merely displays of sexual, intimate or private matters.[46] A Lithuanian Member of Parliament has also stated: "I am not against gays, but I wish they would not demonstrate their views."[47]

Several surveys show that people believe that LGBT persons should not be visible in public, but rather be discreet or confine themselves to the private sphere. For example, according to a study from the Netherlands, 40% of the population find it objectionable if two men kiss in public and 27% feel the same if two women kiss each other. People are much less troubled by a heterosexual couple kissing in public, with 13% taking exception to this. One in three people in the Netherlands find it less problematic if a man and a woman walk hand in hand compared with when two men do the same.[48] A study in Germany shows similar results.[49]

Where LGB persons may have the possibility to choose to be invisible, transgender persons may have the opposite problem. Owing to often long gender reassignment treatment, transgender persons may fall out of the normative perception of what "men" and "women" should look like, which may lead to ridicule and rejection in public. This may also happen during simple everyday occurrences such as not being addressed with the right personal pronoun in shops or banks or when transgender persons use the toilet which fits their gender identity. The lack of positive role models of transgender persons in society further increases the negative attitudes towards this group.

Harsh reactions against LGBT persons are not least seen in relation to the public presence of LGBT persons, for example during Pride parades. Fierce reactions against public LGBT demonstrations in many member states show that homophobic and transphobic expressions are particularly accentuated when LGBT persons are visible in public – either as individuals or as

---

46. National contribution (sociological report) on Azerbaijan, p. 7; National contribution (sociological report) on Ukraine, p. 6.
47. Lithuanian tabloid *LT* (13 February 2007) quoted in Terškinas A., "Not Private Enough? Homophobic and Injurious Speech in the Lithuanian Media", LGL, Vilnius, 2008, p. 10.
48. Keuzenkamp S., "Steeds gewoner, nooit gewoon. Acceptatie van homoseksualiteit in Nederland", Sociaal en Cultureel Planbureau, The Hague, 2010, pp. 355-56.
49. Institut für interdisziplinäre Konflikt und Gewaltforschung, "Indikatoren des Syndroms Gruppenbezogene Menschenfeindlichkeit im Vergleich", 2006, p. 17.

groups claiming their right to freedom of assembly. The visibility of LGBT persons and the public character of such events appear to increase the level of general reactions and expression of attitudes in both negative and positive terms.

1.6. Media

The media have a significant influence on, and to some extent mirror, public opinion and attitudes in society. In a majority of member states, among others in the United Kingdom, Denmark, Luxembourg, Portugal and Germany, reports from LGBT organisations and surveys[50] show that LGBT issues lack presence in the media and that the media, to varying degrees, simplify, sensationalise and stereotype LGBT persons and the issues crucial for them. A Slovenian study[51] carried out a comprehensive analysis of the Slovenian print media from 1970 to 2000, in which five dominant categories of LGB images were identified:

– stereotyping – relying on rigid gender schemes presenting gay men as effeminate and lesbian women as masculine;

– medicalisation – consigning homosexuality to the medical and psychiatric spheres and searching for causes;

– sexualisation – reducing homosexuality to a question of sex;

– secrecy – making homosexuality appear as concealed and related to shame and regret;

– normalisation – making homosexuals appear as heterosexuals in order to make homosexuality less threatening and politicised.

A study in the United Kingdom called negative and inaccurate representations of transgender persons "an endemic problem, leading to considerable suffering on the part of transgender persons".[52] It also suggested that such representations inspired at least some verbal and physical abuse against transgender persons. Transgender persons face the problem of "medicalisation of identity" and the medical labels applied to them, not only by the medical profession and public officials but also by society at large. A study from

---

50. Stonewall, "Written Out: The Scottish Press' Portrayal of Lesbian, Gay, Bisexual and Transgender People", Scotland, 2007; FRA national contribution (sociological report) on Luxembourg, p. 8; FRA national contribution (sociological report) on Denmark, p. 10; FRA national contribution (sociological report) on Portugal, pp. 8-9; Walters S. D., "Take my Domestic Partner, Please: Gays and Marriage in the Era of the Visible", 2001, in Bernstein M. and Reimann R. (eds), *Queer families, Queer Politics: Challenging Culture and the State*, Columbia UP, New York, pp. 338-57.
51. Kuhar R., *Media Representations of Homosexuality: An Analysis of the Print Media in Slovenia, 1970-2000*, Mediawatch: Ljubljana, 2003, p. 7, also quoted in European Union Agency for Fundamental Human Rights, "Homophobia and Discrimination on Grounds of Sexual Orientation and Gender Identity in the European Union Member States: Part II – The Social Situation", 2009, p. 92.
52. Trans Media Watch, "How Transgender People Experience the Media. Conclusions from Research November 2009-February 2010", 2010, p. 11.

Belgium[53] found hardly any media focus on transgender issues apart from a sensationalist or medical perspective. Evidence showing that lesbian, bisexual and transgender persons are more invisible than gay men in the media has been reported in many member states, including Austria, the Czech Republic, Portugal, Slovenia, Sweden and the United Kingdom.[54]

A particular problem is homophobic and transphobic discourse in the media. This has been identified as a problem in many member states, including in Bosnia and Herzegovina, Italy, Poland and Latvia.[55] Incidents have been reported in studies from Lithuania, Germany, Scotland (United Kingdom) and "the former Yugoslav Republic of Macedonia". Some studies, such as one in Bosnia and Herzegovina, go as far as to conclude that the media are perceived "as the most public promoter of homophobia, also by using language of hate".[56] The media as an active player in the creation of negative perceptions of LGBT people was also found in an analysis of the Russian media.[57]

On the positive side, some studies demonstrate that there is an increased presence and a more nuanced presentation of LGBT persons in the media in some member states. A study in the Czech Republic found that "while in the first half of the 1990s negative stereotyping, sexualisation and comedic or criminal contexts were dominant factors in LGBT representation", coverage of LGBT persons in the media increasingly improved afterwards.[58] A study on media representations of LGBT persons in "the former Yugoslav Republic of Macedonia" also found that even though the media still, to some extent, portray LGBT persons in an excessively sexualised manner, the situation has changed drastically in the period 2000-2009, influenced by the emergence of new media and LGBT activism.[59] In a Spanish[60] study some objective and balanced coverage of LGBT topics in the media has been reported In Lithuania, a LGBT organisation worked closely with the media to provide

---

53. FRA national contribution (sociological report) on Belgium, p. 9.
54. FRA national contribution (sociological report) on Czech Republic, p. 9; FRA national contribution (sociological report) on Austria, p. 9; FRA national contribution (sociological report) on Portugal, pp. 8-9; FRA national contribution (sociological report) on Slovenia, p. 9; FRA national contribution (sociological report) on Sweden, p. 10; FRA national contribution (sociological report) on the United Kingdom, p. 11.
55. National contribution (sociological report) on Bosnia and Herzegovina, pp. 12-13; FRA national contribution (sociological report) on Latvia, p. 12; FRA national contribution (sociological report) on Poland, p. 10; FRA national contribution (sociological report) on Italy, p. 11.
56. Organization Q, "The Invisible Q? Human Rights Issues and Concerns of LGBTIQ Persons in Bosnia and Herzegovina", Sarajevo, 2008, p. 50.
57. Moscow Helsinki Group, "Situation of Lesbians, Gays, Bisexuals and Transgenders in the Russian Federation", 2009, pp. 52-57.
58. Working Group on the Issues of Sexual Minorities of the Minister for Human Rights and National Minorities, "Analysis of the Situation of the Lesbian, Gay, Bisexual and Transgender Minority in the Czech Republic", Government of Czech Republic, 2007, pp. 49-51, also quoted in European Union Agency for Fundamental Human Rights, "Homophobia and Discrimination on Grounds of Sexual Orientation and Gender Identity in the European Union Member States: Part II – The Social Situation", 2009, p. 93.
59. Dimitrov S., "Sexualities in Transition: Discourses, Power and Sexual Minorities in Transitional Macedonia", Euro-Balkan – Institute for Humanities and Social Science research, Skopje, 2009, p. 88.
60. FRA national contribution (sociological report) on Spain, p. 9.

journalists with training and tools to improve reporting on LGBT issues.[61] Some improved media coverage on LGBT issues has also been reported by NGOs in Albania, Croatia, Moldova, Montenegro, Serbia and Turkey though serious problems remain.

The presence of positive role models in the media was highlighted by many interlocutors as being of paramount importance for the visibility of LGBT persons. Role models could include openly LGBT artists, opinion leaders, sportspersons or politicians. Other good practices can also be reported in this field. In 2005 in the Russian Federation, the Institute of Press Development organised two educational seminars for journalists in St Petersburg. The seminars served the purpose of dismantling myths and stereotypes about LGBT persons, and they allowed journalists to ask questions to representatives of the LGBT community.[62] NGOs in other member states have also conducted such workshops for journalists. Another good practice is reported about the broadcaster Channel 4 in the United Kingdom which actively monitors how the channel portrays ethnic minority groups, gays and lesbians, people with disabilities, and other groups. For that purpose, it conducts ongoing audience reputation tracking surveys and commissioned a study in 2009 on viewers' perceptions of the representation and portrayal of lesbian women and gay men.[63]

---

61. Lithuanian Gay League, "A Media for Diversity: LGBT in the News – A Guide for Better Reporting".
62. Sabynaeva M., "Lesbians, Gays, Journalists: In Search for Mutual Understanding", November 2005.
63. Channel Four Television Corporation, "Report and Financial Statements 2009", 2010, p. 50.

2. Legal standards and their implementation

2.1. Introduction

In debates on the human rights of LGBT persons it is sometimes assumed that the protection of the human rights of lesbian, gay, bisexual and transgender people amounts to introducing new rights or "special" rights. This line of thinking is misleading, as international human rights law clearly recognises that all human beings, irrespective of their sexual orientation or gender identity, are entitled to all rights and freedoms deriving from the inherent dignity of the human person without discrimination. Legislative and judicial developments in the last decades have led to the consistent interpretation that sexual orientation and gender identity are recognised as prohibited grounds of discrimination under major human rights treaties and conventions, including the UN International Covenants and the European Convention on Human Rights. This chapter outlines the agreed universal standards from the perspective of non-discrimination followed by a summary of the relevant national legal frameworks. The implementation of the legal standards by national structures for promoting equality and the means of national policy initiatives is also highlighted.

2.2. International and European standards

UN instruments

The principles of equality in dignity and rights and non-discrimination are fundamental elements of international human rights law. These principles are enshrined in the Universal Declaration of Human Rights and reiterated as legally binding obligations in the UN International Covenants. Thus, Article 2(1) of the International Covenant of Civil and Political Rights (ICCPR) and Article 2(2) of the International Covenant on Economic, Social and Cultural Rights (ICESCR) oblige states to ensure the enjoyment of human rights without any discrimination on grounds of race, colour, sex, language, religion, political or other opinion, national or social origin, property, birth or other status. The principle of non-discrimination before the law is laid down in Article 26 of the ICCPR and prohibits discrimination on the same grounds listed in Article 2(1) of the ICCPR.

Although sexual orientation and gender identity are not expressly mentioned as prohibited grounds of discrimination, the respective treaty bodies have interpreted the covenants in their case law[64] or in a general comment as including sexual orientation and gender identity within the scope of the open-ended lists of grounds. Indeed, in its General Comment No. 20, the UN

---

64. UN Human Rights Committee, *Toonen v. Australia*, Communication No. 488/1992 30, March 1994, CCPR/C/50/D/488/1992, paragraph 8.7; UN Human Rights Committee, *Young v. Australia*, Communication No. 941/2000, 6 August 2003, CCPR/C/78/D/941/2000; UN Human Rights Committee, *X v. Colombia*, Communication No. 1361/2005, 14 May 2007, CCPR/C/89/D/1361/2005.

Committee on Economic, Social and Cultural Rights explains that the "States Parties should ensure that a person's sexual orientation is not a barrier to realising Covenant rights, for example, in accessing survivor's pension rights. In addition, gender identity is recognised as among the prohibited grounds of discrimination; for example, persons who are transgender, transsexual or intersex often face serious human rights violations, such as harassment in schools or in the workplace."[65]

The principle of non-discrimination is also part of more specialised UN human rights conventions. The UN Convention on Elimination of All Forms of Discrimination against Women (CEDAW) contains a non-discrimination clause[66] and the Committee on the Elimination of Discrimination Against Women has clarified in a general recommendation that "discrimination of women based on sex and gender is inextricably linked with other factors that affect women, such as race, ethnicity, religion or belief, health, status, age, class, caste, and sexual orientation and gender identity. ... States Parties must legally recognize and prohibit such intersecting forms of discrimination and their compounded negative impact on the women concerned."[67] Similarly, Article 2 of the UN Convention on the Rights of the Child (CRC) constitutes a general non-discrimination provision for the enjoyment of the rights protected under the convention. In a general comment, the Committee on the Rights of the Child referred specifically to sexual orientation as a prohibited ground of discrimination, albeit not gender identity.[68]

Several UN special rapporteurs have applied the international standards in raising serious human rights concerns about the treatment of LGBT persons. They include the Special Rapporteur on the Right to Freedom of Opinion and Expression,[69] the Special Rapporteur on the Right of Everyone to the Enjoyment of the Highest Attainable Standard of Physical and Mental Health,[70] the Special Rapporteur on the Right to Education,[71] the Special Rapporteur on Adequate Housing as a Component of the Right to an Adequate Standard of Living[72]

---

65. UN Committee on Economic, Social and Cultural Rights, General Comment No. 20 on Non-Discrimination in relation to Economic, Social and Cultural Rights, 2009, paragraph 32.
66. Convention on the Elimination of All Forms of Discrimination against Women, 1979, Article 2.
67. General Recommendation No. 28 on the core obligations of states parties under Article 2 of the Convention on the Elimination of All Forms of Discrimination against Women, CEDAW/C/2010/47/GC.2, paragraph 18.
68. UN Committee on the Rights of the Child, General Comment No. 4, 2003, paragraph 6.
69. United Nations, "Report of the Special Rapporteur on the Right to Freedom of Opinion and Expression, Ambeyi Ligabo, Addendum: Mission to Columbia", E/CN.4/2005/64/Add.3 of 26 November 2004, paragraph 75.
70. United Nations, "The Right of Everyone to the Enjoyment of the Highest Attainable Standard of Physical and Mental Health – Report of the Special Rapporteur, Paul Hunt", E/CN.4/2004/49, paragraph 24; Human Rights Council, "Report of the Special Rapporteur on the Right of Everyone to the Enjoyment of the Highest Attainable Standard of Physical and Mental Health, Anand Grover", A/HRC/14/20, paragraph 9, 27 April 2010.
71. United Nations, Commission on Human Rights, "Economic, Social and Cultural Rights, Girls' Right to Education, Report Submitted by the Special Rapporteur on the Right to Education, Mr V. Muñoz Villalobos", 8 February 2006, paragraph 113; United Nations, "Report of the United Nations Special Rapporteur on the Right to Education", A/65/162, 23 July 2010, paragraph 23.
72. UN Economic and Social Council, "Report of the Special Rapporteur on Adequate Housing as a Component of the Right to an Adequate Standard of Living, Miloon Kothari", E/CN.4/2004/48, 8 March 2004, paragraph 49.

and the Special Rapporteur on the Question of Torture and Other Cruel, Inhuman or Degrading Treatment or Punishment.[73]

Council of Europe instruments

All member states of the Council of Europe are parties to the European Convention on Human Rights. The Convention provides an open-ended list of grounds in Article 14 on the prohibition of discrimination, which are repeated in Protocol No. 12 to the Convention on the general prohibition of discrimination. The Protocol has a wider scope of application than Article 14 since its scope of application is not limited to the rights and freedoms set out in the Convention itself. Neither Article 14 nor the Protocol specifically mentions sexual orientation or gender identity as prohibited discrimination grounds but the commentary on the provisions of the said Protocol stipulates that the list of non-discrimination grounds is not exhaustive.[74]

The European Court of Human Rights confirmed in 1999 that sexual orientation is a discrimination ground covered by Article 14 of the Convention.[75] Similarly, in 2010, the Court explicitly mentioned transsexuality[76] – albeit not gender identity – as a prohibited ground of discrimination under Article 14 of the Convention although this could have been adduced from its earlier rulings as well.[77] The Court has issued several landmark judgments on alleged discrimination on grounds of sexual orientation in which Article 14 has been invoked in conjunction with substantive articles of the Convention, in particular Article 8 on the right to respect for private and family life. In these cases, the Court has severely limited the margin of appreciation of states stressing that differences in treatment related to this ground require particularly weighty reasons to be legitimate under the Convention.[78]

The principle of non-discrimination can also be found in more specialised Council of Europe conventions. On 7 April 2011, the Committee of Ministers adopted the Convention on preventing and combating

---

73. "Report of the United Nations Special Rapporteur on the Question of Torture and Other Cruel, Inhuman or Degrading Treatment or Punishment", UN Doc. A/56/156, 3 July 2001, paragraph 22; UN General Assembly, UN Doc. A/59/324, 1 September 2004, paragraph 39.
74. Explanatory report to Protocol No. 12 to the 1950 Convention for the Protection of Human Rights and Fundamental Freedoms, which entered into force on 1 April 2005, ETS No. 177.
75. See European Court of Human Rights, *Mouta v. Portugal*, Application No. 33290/96, judgment of 21 December 1999. However, as early as 1981 the Court had found in *Dudgeon v. United Kingdom*, Application No. 7525/76, that discrimination in the criminal law regarding consenting relations between same-sex adults in private was contrary to the right to respect for private life in Article 8 ECHR.
76. European Court of Human Rights, *P.V. v. Spain*, Application No. 35159/09, judgment of 30 November 2010, paragraph 30. In the specific case no violation of the provision was found. Judgment not final.
77. See for example European Court of Human Rights, *Christine Goodwin v. United Kingdom*, Application No. 28957/95, judgment of 11 July 2002.
78. European Court of Human Rights, *Karner v. Austria*, Application No. 40016/98, judgment of 24 July 2003, paragraph 37, *E. B. v France*, Application No. 43546/02, judgment of 22 January 2008, paragraph 91 and *Schalk and Kopf v. Austria*, Application No. 30141/04, judgment of 24 June 2010, paragraph 97.

violence against women and domestic violence.[79] This convention is the first legally binding instrument in the world creating a comprehensive legal framework to prevent violence and to protect victims. The non-discrimination article of the convention includes the grounds of sexual orientation and gender identity thereby making it the first international treaty to include explicitly both sexual orientation and gender identity as prohibited grounds of discrimination.

Another binding Council of Europe instrument, the revised European Social Charter, includes an open-ended non-discrimination provision in Article E with reference to the enjoyment of the rights set out in the charter. Although sexual orientation and gender identity are not directly mentioned among the prohibited grounds of discrimination, in 2009, the European Committee of Social Rights affirmed that educational materials should not reinforce demeaning stereotypes and prejudice which contribute to the social exclusion, discrimination and denial of human dignity often experienced by historically marginalised groups such as persons of non-heterosexual orientation.[80]

In 2010, the Council of Europe Committee of Ministers adopted a Recommendation on measures to combat discrimination on grounds of sexual orientation or gender identity.[81] The recommendation invites the member states to ensure that the stipulated principles and measures are applied in national legislation, policies and practices relevant to the protection of the human rights of LGBT persons. The recommendation covers a wide range of areas including hate crime, freedoms of association, expression and peaceful assembly, respect for family life and private life, employment, education, health, housing, sports, asylum, national human rights structures and discrimination on multiple grounds. While it is not a legally binding instrument, all Council of Europe member states should implement this recommendation. The Parliamentary Assembly of the Council of Europe also adopted resolutions and recommendations on the subject.[82]

---

79. The convention was opened for signature in Istanbul on 11 May 2011 (CETS No. 210).
80. See European Committee of Social Rights, *International Centre for the Legal Protection of Human Rights (Interights) v. Croatia* – Collective Complaint No. 45/2007, decision of 30 March 2009, paragraphs 60-61.
81. See Committee of Ministers Recommendation CM/Rec(2010)5 on measures to combat discrimination on grounds of sexual orientation or gender identity – Explanatory Memorandum to the Recommendation, CM(2010)4 add3 rev2E, 29 March 2010.
82. Recommendation 1915 (2010) of the Parliamentary Assembly on Discrimination on the basis of sexual orientation and gender identity; Resolution 1728 (2010) of the Parliamentary Assembly on Discrimination on the basis of sexual orientation and gender identity; Recommendation 1635 (2003) of the Parliamentary Assembly on Lesbians and gays in sport; Recommendation 1474 (2000) of the Parliamentary Assembly on situation of lesbians and gays in Council of Europe member states; Recommendation 1470 (2000) of the Parliamentary Assembly on Situation of gays and lesbians and their partners in respect of asylum and immigration in the member states of the Council of Europe; Recommendation 1117 (1989) of the Parliamentary Assembly on the condition of transsexuals; Recommendation 924 (1981) of the Parliamentary Assembly on Discrimination against homosexuals; Resolution 756 (1981) of the Parliamentary Assembly on discrimination against homosexuals.

European Union instruments

Currently, 27 member states of the Council of Europe are also members of the European Union. The general principle of equal treatment between men and women was introduced into European Union law in 1957 by the Treaty Establishing the European Economic Community (the Treaty of Rome). The Treaty of Amsterdam (1997) and the Treaty of Lisbon (2007) further strengthened the equal treatment principle by allowing European Union measures to combat discrimination on several grounds, including sexual orientation albeit not gender identity. The Treaty on European Union (TEU) as modified by the Lisbon Treaty affirms the centrality of "respect for human dignity, freedom, democracy, equality, the rule of law and respect for human rights, including the rights of persons belonging to minorities"[83] as a fundamental principle of the Union. These values are also deemed essential for a society in which non-discrimination prevails. Accordingly, the Lisbon Treaty renders the principle of non-discrimination into a horizontal clause which should apply in the implementation of the entire text of the treaty.

The Charter of Fundamental Rights of the European Union includes a general non-discrimination provision in Article 21.1 of the charter that also mentions sexual orientation among the prohibited grounds of discrimination.[84] Gender identity is not explicitly mentioned but since the list of grounds is not exhaustive it is open for the inclusion of other grounds that give rise to differential treatment. Moreover, the scope of the ground of "sex" in the Charter of Fundamental Rights should be applied in conformity with the jurisprudence of the Court of Justice of the European Union on that ground.

The European Union has also introduced specific equal treatment directives. Currently, combating discrimination on grounds of sexual orientation under European Union law is limited to the field of employment only.[85] The question of extending the material scope of the principle of equal treatment between persons irrespective of sexual orientation beyond employment is being examined by the Council of the European Union with reference to a Commission proposal for a so-called "horizontal" equal treatment directive.[86]

Gender identity is not explicitly recognised as a prohibited ground of discrimination in the European Union directives. However, the Court of Justice of the European Union has applied the ground of sex to extend equal treatment guarantees to cover, at least partially, the discrimination experienced

---

83. European Union, Consolidated Version of the Treaty on European Union, OJ C115/13, Article 2, 9 May 2008.
84. Charter of Fundamental Rights of the European Union, adopted in 2000, OJ C 83/02, 30 March 2010.
85. European Union, Council Directive 2000/78/EC of 27 November 2000, establishing a general framework for equal treatment in employment and occupation, 2000, OJ 2000 L 303. See also Court of Justice of the European Union, C-267/06, *Tadao Maruko v. Versorgungsanstalt der deutschen Bühnen VddB*, judgment of 1 April 2008, paragraph 65, ECR I-1757.
86. European Union, Proposal for a Council Directive on implementing the principle of equal treatment between persons irrespective of religion or belief, disability, age or sexual orientation COM/2008/0426 final – 2008/0140 (CNS), 2 July 2008.

by transgender persons. In the case of *P. v. S. and Cornwall County Council* from 1996, the Court of Justice stated that the principle of equal treatment "must extend to discrimination arising from gender reassignment, which is based, essentially if not exclusively, on the sex of the person concerned, since to dismiss a person on the ground that he or she intends to undergo, or has undergone, gender reassignment is to treat him or her unfavourably by comparison with persons of the sex to which he or she was deemed to belong before that operation".[87] This was confirmed by two other decisions of the Court of Justice.[88] In line with this jurisprudence, the Council of the European Union has stated that discrimination arising from gender reassignment is also protected under the scope of the European Union Directive implementing the principle of equal treatment between men and women in the access to and supply of goods and services.[89] The Gender Recast Directive of 2006 became the first European Union Directive which also refers to persons intending to undergo or having undergone gender reassignment.[90]

Whereas European Union law thus protects this segment of the transgender community under the ground of "sex", European Union law does not explicitly cover the right to equal treatment of transgender people who have not undergone and do not intend to undergo gender reassignment surgery. In June 2010, the European Parliament called upon the European Commission to ensure that future European Union gender equality initiatives address this gap.[91] The European Commission has decided to examine "specific issues pertaining to sex discrimination in relation to gender identity" in the framework of the European Union's Strategy for equality between women and men 2010-2015.[92]

Yogyakarta Principles

The Yogyakarta Principles on the Application of International Human Rights Law in relation to Sexual Orientation and Gender Identity, adopted in 2006 by a group of human rights experts, promote the implementation of already existing obligations under international human rights law in relation to LGBT persons. As such, they propose baseline standards for the protection and

---

87. Court of Justice of the European Union, C-13/94, *P. v. S. and Cornwall County Council*, judgment of 30 April 1996, paragraphs 21-22.
88. Court of Justice of the European Union, C-117/01, *K.B. v. National Health Service Pensions Agency, Secretary of State for Health*, judgment of 7 January 2004, C-423/04, *Sarah Margaret Richards v. Secretary of State for Work and Pensions*, judgment of 27 April 2006.
89. 2606th meeting of the Council of the European Union (Employment, Social Policy, Health and Consumers Affairs) held in Luxembourg on 4 October 2004, Minutes, Doc. No. 13369/04 of 27 October 2004, p. 7.
90. European Union, Directive 2006/54/EC of the European Parliament and of the Council of 5 July 2006 on the implementation of the principle of equal opportunities and equal treatment of men and women in matters of employment and occupation (recast) OJ L 204, 26 June 2006 pp. 23-36. Recital No. 3.
91. European Parliament Resolution of 17 June 2010 on assessment of the results of the 2006-2010 Roadmap for Equality between women and men, and forward-looking recommendations.
92. Communication from the Commission to the Council, the European Parliament, the European Economic and Social Committee and the Committee of the Regions: Strategy for equality between women and men 2010-2015, paragraph 6.2.

promotion of the full enjoyment of all human rights irrespective of sexual orientation and gender identity. Several states, including the Czech Republic, Denmark, Finland, Iceland, Norway, Sweden and Switzerland, have endorsed the Principles or referred to them in their statements at the United Nations Human Rights Council. Other countries endorsed the principles at the executive level (Germany, the Netherlands, Spain and the United Kingdom) or the legislative level (Belgium).[93]

2.3. National standards

Non-discrimination legislation at the national level has developed at great speed during recent decades. Most member states of the Council of Europe have now adopted non-discrimination legislation. In some countries this is a recent phenomenon while in others national non-discrimination legislation has already been subject to frequent amendments and improvements.

A great number of member states have chosen to introduce a comprehensive prohibition against discrimination. Comprehensive non-discrimination legislation refers to non-discrimination legislation which covers several grounds of discrimination (for example sex or gender, race, religion or belief, age, disability, sexual orientation, gender identity or other status) and provides protection against discrimination on these grounds in several different fields (for example employment, access to goods and services, education, social security and health care). For the purposes of this chapter, national non-discrimination legislation is described as comprehensive when more grounds than sex and race are covered and when the material scope is extended beyond the fields of employment and access to goods and services. Comprehensive non-discrimination legislation can be distinguished from non-discrimination legislation which is specific to a particular field, such as non-discrimination legislation which only applies in the field of employment. This will be referred to in this chapter as sectoral non-discrimination legislation. Third, specialised legislation in different fields may also include non-discrimination provisions, although such legislation does not directly amount to non-discrimination legislation.

Comprehensive non-discrimination legislation

Twenty member states have enacted comprehensive non-discrimination legislation which explicitly includes sexual orientation among the prohibited grounds of discrimination. This is the case in Albania, Belgium, Bosnia and Herzegovina, Bulgaria, Croatia, the Czech Republic, Germany, Hungary, Iceland, Ireland, Montenegro, the Netherlands, Norway, Romania, Serbia, Slovakia, Slovenia, Spain, Sweden and the United Kingdom.

---

93. Ettelbrick P. L. and Zerán A. T., *The Impact of the Yogyakarta Principles on International Human Rights Law Development. A Study of November 2007 – June 2010*, Final Report, 2010, p. 12.

Nine member states (Albania, Croatia, the Czech Republic, Germany, Hungary, Montenegro, Serbia, Sweden and the United Kingdom) have included gender identity explicitly in comprehensive non-discrimination legislation. However, no standard wording is currently followed to cover gender identity in these member states, which may imply significant differences as to the legal scope of these terms.[94] At least 11 member states treat discrimination on grounds of gender identity or gender reassignment as a form of sex or gender discrimination in comprehensive non-discrimination legislation (Andorra, Austria, Belgium, Denmark, Finland, France, Ireland, the Netherlands, Norway, Slovakia and Switzerland), while Sweden[95] has chosen a multiple formulation to describe the applicable ground. In the remaining 27 member states the situation regarding coverage of transgender persons under comprehensive non-discrimination legislation is unclear. These 27 member states include many European Union member states which, under European Union law, should provide protection against discrimination in the fields of employment and access to and supply of goods and services to a person who intends to undergo or has undergone gender reassignment as a form of sex or gender discrimination. However, the FRA has pointed out that the Gender Recast Directive has not yet led to a clear picture regarding the explicit coverage of transgender persons within the realm of non-discrimination legislation in these European Union member states.[96]

Finally, it should be noted that in member states where sexual orientation or gender identity are not explicitly mentioned as prohibited grounds in comprehensive non-discrimination legislation, these grounds may still be covered under "other status" (non-exhaustive list of grounds), possibly explicitly recognised through case law. However, in many other countries this is not clear because case law on discrimination on grounds of sexual orientation and gender identity is scarce.

Sectoral non-discrimination legislation

Several member states which have not enacted comprehensive non-discrimination legislation which prohibits discrimination on the grounds of sexual orientation have enacted sectoral non-discrimination legislation which provides protection on the ground of sexual orientation in the fields of employment and/or access to goods and services. Sexual orientation is an

---

94. Instead of "gender identity" the legislation in these nine member states may refer to "gender expression", "gender identification", "transgender identity", "gender change", "gender reassignment" or "sexual identity". In Spain, the Constitutional Court established that gender identity is to be read in among the prohibited grounds of discrimination. See European Union Agency for Fundamental Rights, "Homophobia, Transphobia and Discrimination on Grounds of Sexual Orientation and Gender Identity: 2010 Update – Comparative Legal Analysis", Vienna, 2010, pp. 21-23.
95. Legislation in Sweden prohibits discrimination on grounds of "transgender identity and expression" and also recognises discrimination of transsexual persons under the ground of "sex".
96. European Union Agency for Fundamental Rights, "Homophobia, Transphobia and Discrimination on Grounds of Sexual Orientation and Gender Identity. 2010 Update-Comparative Legal Analysis", 2010, pp. 21-22.

explicitly prohibited ground of discrimination in sectoral non-discrimination legislation in the fields of employment and access to goods and services in seven member states (Andorra, Austria, Finland, Latvia, Lithuania, Luxembourg and Switzerland). Sexual orientation is an explicitly prohibited ground of discrimination in sectoral non-discrimination legislation in the area of employment, but not with respect to access to goods and services, in 11 member states: Cyprus, Denmark, Estonia, France, Georgia, Greece, Italy, Malta, Poland, Portugal and "the former Yugoslav Republic of Macedonia".[97]

The total number of member states which include sexual orientation either under comprehensive or sectoral non-discrimination legislation is thus 38 (see Map 2.1). Nine member states (Armenia, Azerbaijan, Liechtenstein, Moldova, Monaco, Russian Federation, San Marino, Turkey and Ukraine) have neither sectoral nor comprehensive non-discrimination legislation covering sexual orientation.

Although gender identity or gender reassignment does not appear to be expressly mentioned in sectoral non-discrimination legislation in member states, this ground may still be covered under "other status" (non-exhaustive list of grounds) or under the "sex" or "gender" ground.

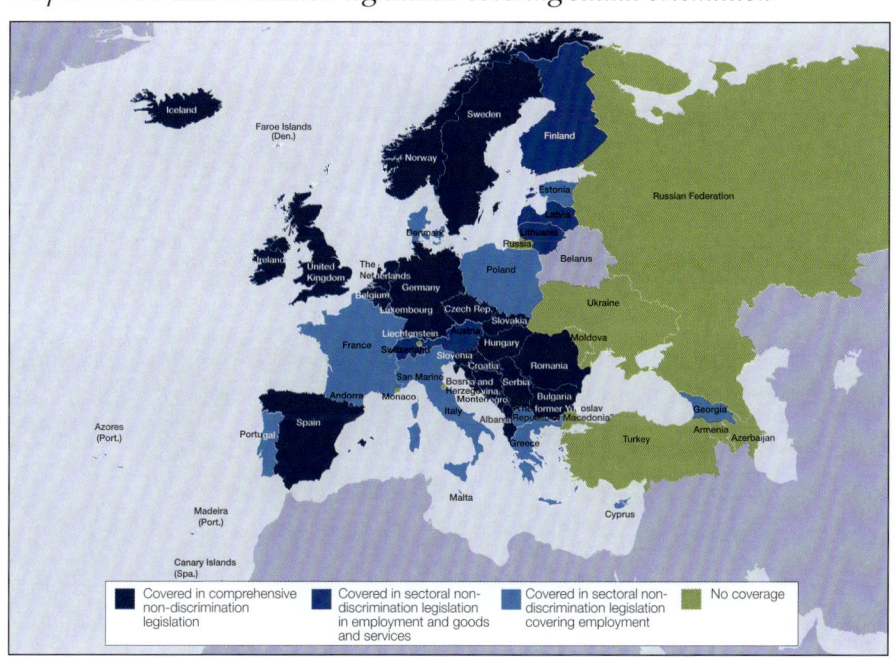

Map 2.1: Non-discrimination legislation covering sexual orientation

---

[97]. Portugal explicitly mentions sexual orientation as a prohibited ground of discrimination in the constitution, Article 13.2.

In at least 20 member states comprehensive or sectoral non-discrimination legislation thus covers transgender persons either on the ground of "sex" or on the ground of "gender identity" albeit in no standard wording (see Map 2.2). For the remaining member states the non-discrimination legislation or its implementation is unclear on this point.

Specialised legislation with a non-discrimination provision

Finally, several member states have specialised legislation in different fields, which includes non-discrimination provisions prohibiting discrimination on the ground of sexual orientation or gender identity. By way of example, in Georgia, the Law on the Rights of the Patient (Article 6) as well as the Law on the Protection of Health (Article 6) explicitly prohibit discrimination due to sexual orientation.[98] In addition to the comprehensive Anti-Discrimination Law, adopted in March 2009, the Serbian Parliament has adopted four laws which specifically ban discrimination based on sexual orientation: the Labour Law, the Law on Higher Education, the Law on Public Information and the Law on Broadcasting.[99] Norway has several specific acts in the field of housing: the Tenancy Act, the Housing Association Act, and the Residential Building Association Act all prohibit discrimination on the basis of sexual orientation and gender when renting out or selling residences.[100]

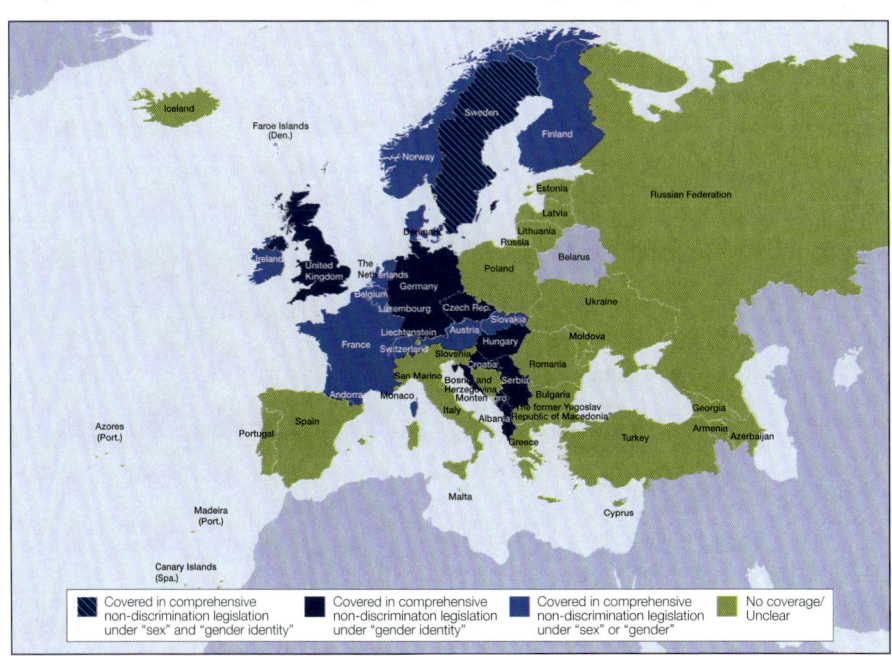

Map 2.2: Non-discrimination legislation covering transgender persons

---

98. National contribution (legal report) on Georgia, p. 5.
99. National contribution (legal report) on Serbia, p. 3.
100. National contribution (legal report) on Norway, p. 4.

Data on cases of discrimination on grounds of sexual orientation or gender identity

Despite the adoption of non-discrimination legislation in many Council of Europe member states, it has been difficult to identify comprehensive data on the application of such laws. This report identified a number of court cases related to alleged discrimination of LGBT persons either under non-discrimination legislation or other legal provisions as well as complaints submitted to national structures promoting equality. Such information on sexual orientation or gender identity discrimination has been identified in 31 member states in the period 2004 to 2010: Austria, Belgium, Bulgaria, Croatia, Cyprus, the Czech Republic, Denmark, Estonia, Finland, France, Georgia, Germany, Greece, Hungary, Iceland, Italy, Latvia, Malta, Moldova, the Netherlands, Norway, Poland, Romania, the Russian Federation, Serbia, Spain, Sweden, Switzerland, Turkey, Ukraine and the United Kingdom.[101] Cases reported by NGOs (but not officially reported by the victim to national structures promoting equality or court) are not included in this list of countries.

Statistics are often not available or not disaggregated by area of discrimination or on the prohibited ground. The lack of information on case law related to discrimination on grounds of sexual orientation or gender identity in the remaining 16 member states may partly be ascribed to the fact that the laws are relatively new for some member states. Other reasons reported by interlocutors include the widespread anti-LGBT public discourse; a lack of awareness raising and training of officials in the area of non-discrimination and the lack of trust in authorities and the judiciary by LGBT victims of discrimination. Moreover, LGBT victims of discrimination often do not want to run the risk of exposure brought about by reporting a case to relevant authorities.

2.4. National structures for promoting equality

National structures for promoting equality are bodies created by statute to promote equality and combat discrimination at member state level. They are usually established under non-discrimination legislation and should carry out their functions independently of all stakeholders, including the state. There is a broad diversity of national structures for promoting equality across the member states. This diversity is particularly evident in the legal structure of the bodies, in the range of grounds that they cover, in the nature of the functions and powers accorded to the bodies, and in the scale of operations of the bodies. Some of these structures are referred to as national equality bodies, others are ombudsmen or national human rights institutions.

There are two broad types of national structures for promoting equality. There are quasi-judicial type bodies which predominantly operate to investigate, hear or mediate, and make findings in relation to claims of discrimination. There are also promotional type bodies that predominantly operate to provide assistance to individuals experiencing discrimination and to implement a broader range

---

101. (FRA) national contributions (legal reports) contain annexes with descriptions on court cases identified in the member states.

of awareness-raising initiatives, survey work and activities supporting good practice. Some national structures have the characteristics of both types.

Within the Council of Europe, the European Commission against Racism and Intolerance (ECRI) has called on national authorities to set up specific national bodies to combat racism, xenophobia, anti-Semitism and other forms of intolerance. ECRI Policy Recommendations No. 2 and No. 7 set out basic principles as guidelines for the establishment and operation of such bodies which should be set up on a constitutional or statutory basis.[102] The Commissioner for Human Rights has issued an Opinion on National Structures for Promoting Equality which gives guidance to member states on enacting comprehensive equal treatment legislation and setting up independent bodies for promoting equality.[103]

Under European Union law, three equality directives (the Race Equality Directive, the Gender Goods and Services Directive and the Gender Recast Directive) require member states of the European Union to establish or designate a body or bodies for the promotion of equal treatment on the grounds of racial or ethnic origin and gender. Although the European Union provisions for establishing equality bodies are limited to race, ethnic origin and gender, several European Union and other member states have enacted non-discrimination legislation and established national structures for promoting equality that clearly go beyond the minimum requirements stipulated by European Union legislation. In practice, most equality bodies set up through the implementation of European Union equality directives also cover either all or some of the grounds stipulated in the Employment Equality Directive, including sexual orientation and in some cases gender identity as well.

Equality bodies in 21 European Union countries are vested with the mandate to receive complaints of discrimination on many grounds, including on the grounds of sexual orientation: Austria, Belgium, Bulgaria, Cyprus, Denmark, Estonia, France, Germany, Greece, Hungary, Ireland, Latvia, Lithuania, Luxembourg, the Netherlands, Portugal[104], Romania, Slovakia, Slovenia, Sweden and the United Kingdom. The other six European Union member states do not have any equality body formally competent to address discrimination on grounds of sexual orientation (the Czech Republic, Finland, Italy, Malta,[105] Poland and Spain). However, in four of these, another national human rights structure promoting equality (for example, an ombudsman institution)

---

102. European Commission against Racism and Intolerance, General Policy Recommendation No. 2 on specialised bodies to combat racism, xenophobia, anti-Semitism and intolerance at national level, adopted on 13 June 1997, CRI(97)36; and General Policy Recommendation No. 7 on national legislation to combat racism and racial discrimination, adopted on 13 December 2002, CRI(2003)8.
103. Commissioner for Human Rights, "Opinion on National Structures for Promoting Equality", CommDH(2011)2.
104. In Portugal, the Commission for Citizenship and Gender Equality is the co-ordinating body for implementation of the *National Plan for Equality: Gender, Citizenship and Non-Discrimination 2011-13*. Relevant references are found on pp. 2, 308 and 314-15 of this plan.
105. However, in Malta the National Commission for the Promotion of Equality (NCPE) has initiated a qualitative study on discrimination experienced by LGBT persons.

competent to receive complaints about discrimination on grounds of sexual orientation is in place (the Czech Republic, Finland, Poland and Spain).

As regards the ground of gender identity, the situation is quite varied. At least four equality bodies (Hungary, Slovakia, Sweden and the United Kingdom) have an explicit mandate to cover gender identity as a ground of discrimination. The Commission for Citizenship and Gender Equality in Portugal has also recently started to incorporate issues of gender identity in its activities. In many other countries gender identity may be covered, at least partially, through the ground of sex or gender in line with European Union law. In some countries gender identity may also be addressed among the unspecified grounds of open-ended lists of discrimination grounds in national equal treatment legislation. In a survey on national equality bodies conducted by the European Network of Equality Bodies (Equinet) in 2009, some 25% of the bodies reported that they, in one way or another, actually received and treated complaints related to discrimination on the ground of gender identity.[106] Under European Union law, more equality bodies should join to carry out such work.

In other member states of the Council of Europe there may be different bodies dealing with different grounds of discrimination or bodies with separate functions respecting a division into promotional and quasi-judicial functions. Many of these institutions are ombudsman bodies or national human rights institutions with the mandate to protect and promote human rights, including non-discrimination, with reference to the Paris Principles.[107] Some of them also deal with issues or incidents related to sexual orientation and gender identity.

For example in Croatia, the Office of the People's Ombudsman and the Ombudsperson for Gender Equality are mandated to receive complaints on the grounds of sexual orientation and gender identity under the non-discrimination legislation. In Norway, the Equality and Anti-Discrimination Ombud has the power both to promote equality in society and to enforce non-discrimination legislation, including by treating individual complaints within and outside the labour market with regard to a wide range of discrimination grounds. Sexual orientation is covered as an explicit discrimination ground, whereas gender identity is currently addressed though the ground of gender.

Adoption of new non-discrimination legislation in some member states means that new equality bodies are in the process of being established with a mandate to enforce and monitor the implementation of the legislation. These include the Commissioner for Protection against Discrimination in Albania and the Commissioner for Protection from Discrimination in Serbia. Both of them have an explicit mandate to address discrimination on the grounds of sexual orientation and gender identity.

---

106. Equinet, "Making Equality Legislation work for Trans people", 2010, p. 7.
107. Principles relating to the Status of National Institutions (the Paris Principles), UN General Assembly Resolution 48/134 of 20 December 1993.

National structures for promoting equality possess great potential for dealing with complaints on grounds of sexual orientation and gender identity as well as promoting the enjoyment of human rights by LGBT persons more generally. However, awareness of these possibilities should be enhanced among LGBT communities as well as within national structures themselves. The Human Rights Defender of Armenia, for example, noted that his office receives a large number of complaints about discrimination from minorities but has not registered any from LGBT persons. He concludes that this "is the best proof that the problem is bigger than assumed and well hidden".[108]

Many LGBT NGOs interviewed for this study expressed the view that national structures were not sufficiently active in this field. Although an increasing number of equality bodies, ombudsmen and national human rights institutions appear to work on questions related to sexual orientation and homophobia, even more efforts are needed to initiate work to address discrimination on grounds of gender identity.

2.5. National policy initiatives

Action plans and policy initiatives

Some member states have chosen to integrate the human rights of LGBT persons into general national action plans for human rights and equality. For example in Sweden, the *National Action Plan for Human Rights 2006-2009*[109] included 135 measures, some of which focused on promoting the enjoyment of human rights by LGBT persons. In Portugal, the National Plan for Equality for the first time has a chapter on sexual orientation and gender identity.[110]

Other member states have set up specific national policies or action plans to improve the human rights situation of LGBT persons in their countries. Such initiatives were identified in Norway,[111] Belgium[112] and the Netherlands.[113] In the Netherlands, the policy plan "Simply Gay" constitutes a national action plan encompassing 60 different measures, including 24 projects sponsored or implemented by various government departments. This "mainstreaming" approach aims to ensure that LGBT human rights are taken into account when drafting general equality and human rights policies.

Public policies are also developed and implemented by local or regional authorities. The city councils of Cologne, Turin and Barcelona have developed policies focused on fighting homophobia and transphobia under

---

108. National contribution (sociological report) on Armenia, p. 11.
109. Swedish Government Communication 2005/06:95.
110. National Plan for Equality: Gender, Citizenship and Non-Discrimination 2011-13, Lisbon, 2011, pp. 314-15.
111. Norwegian Ministry of Children and Equality, "The Norwegian Government's action plan – Improving quality of life among lesbians, gays, bisexuals, and transgender persons, 2009-2012", Oslo, 2008.
112. LGBT Policy in Flanders – a brief introduction, Flemish Government, Brussels, 2010.
113. Emancipatienota 'Gewoon homo zijn', Parliamentary Papers II 2007-2008, 27017, No. 3.

the project Against Homophobia European local Administration Devices (AHEAD). The objective of this project is the preparation of a White Book that collects recommendations and good practices to foster local public policies aimed at fighting discrimination on grounds of sexual orientation and gender identity. Similar local or regional policies have also been developed in Berlin, Ghent, Antwerp, and Dumfries and Galloway.[114] In the Netherlands, national government funding is provided through a national expertise centre, which assists civil servants in 18 municipalities to devise policies which aim to improve attitudes towards LGBT people.

Policy initiatives should ideally have a solid knowledge base. A few examples of research commissioned by public authorities in Council of Europe member states were identified during the study. In the Netherlands, research in different subject areas is commissioned to centres of expertise.[115] Two surveys about safety at schools for LGB persons were also conducted by the Netherlands Inspectorate of Schools.[116] In Belgium, the Flemish Policy Research Centre on Equal Opportunities carries out scientific research on equal opportunities issues, which includes a specific line of research on LGBT persons. The University of Ghent and the Flemish authorities' Equal Opportunities Assistance Centre have carried out a study into the school careers of LGB persons.[117] In Italy in 2008 the Minister of Equal Opportunities signed an agreement with the National Statistics Office to carry out the first multipurpose survey regarding "Discrimination on the grounds of sexual orientation, identity and ethnicity".[118]

Governments may also rely on research conducted in co-operation with national structures for promoting equality and develop specific activities based on the outcome of such research. For example, in the United Kingdom the Scottish Government and the Equality and Human Rights Commission have commissioned a discrimination module as part of the Scottish Social Attitudes Survey, which is conducted every four years. The survey includes questions on attitudes towards lesbian, gay and bisexual people and, since 2006, transgender people.[119] In Germany the Federal

---

114. "Building a Network – Roundtable of Local Focal Points LGBT Equality Policies – Rainbow cities", The Hague, 27 October 2010.
115. Research is, for example, conducted in the area of family law (annual statistics about registered partnerships and civil marriages of same-sex couples) collected by the National Statistics Institute, CBS; the Annual National Monitor of criminal cases of discrimination against LGBT persons reported to the Police; further research conducted by the Netherlands Institute for Social Research, SCP and the Netherlands Centre for Social Development, MOVISIE.
116. Netherlands Inspectorate of Schools, Weerbaar en divers, Onderzoek naar seksuele diversiteit en seksuele weerbaarheid in het onderwijs. Anders zijn is van iedereen, 26 February 2009.
117. Dewaele, Cox, Van Houtte & Vincke, De schoolloopbaan van holebi- en heterojongeren. Steunpunt Gelijkekansenbeleid, University Antwerp – University Hasselt, University Ghent. Antwerp, 2008.
118. FRA national contribution (legal report) on Italy, p. 6.
119. Bromley C., Curtice J. and Given L., "Equalities: Research Findings No.1/2007: Attitudes to Discrimination in Scotland 2006: Scottish Social Attitudes Survey", Scottish Centre for Social Research, 2007, Edinburgh; Ormston R., McConville S and Reid S., "Scottish Social Attitudes 2010", Scottish Centre for Social Research, 2010, Edinburgh.

Anti-Discrimination Agency published research on discrimination against transgender people in working life.[120]

Co-ordination and consultation structures

Some member states have set up specific co-ordination and consultation structures within their national administrations regarding LGBT-related policy and legislative initiatives. In Estonia, the Gender Equality Department of the Ministry of Social Affairs has, since 2009, consulted with different LGBT organisations and worked on increasing competence in the field. In Poland, the Department for Women, Family and Counteracting Discrimination of the Polish Ministry of Labour and Social Policy set up an Advisory Committee which included experts on the issue of discrimination on the grounds of sexual orientation.[121]

In Ukraine, the Ministry of the Interior has set up public councils in all regions of the country, in which representatives from civil society and local police officers discuss relevant human rights. The Ukrainian NGO Our World was a member of such a council in the Kiev district, and the NGO For Equal Rights was a member in the Kherson district.[122] Interdepartmental structures were also identified in the Netherlands ("LGBT interdepartmental working group") and the Czech Republic, where a Committee for Sexual Minorities continues the work of a previous working group which made a detailed analysis of the situation of lesbian, gay, bisexual and transgender minorities.[123]

Co-ordination and consultations on national LGBT policies between many member states of the Council of Europe also take place in the European Network of Governmental LGBT Focal Points, which has included government representatives from 23 member states.

---

120. Federal Anti-Discrimination Agency, Benachteiligung von Trans Personen, insbesondere im Arbeitsleben, Berlin, 2010.
121. FRA national contribution (legal report) on Poland, p. 84.
122. National contribution on Ukraine (sociological report), p. 9.
123. Working Group on the Issues of Sexual Minorities of the Minister for Human Rights and National Minorities, "Analysis of the Situation of the Lesbian, Gay, Bisexual and Transgender Minorities in the Czech Republic", 2007.

3. Protection: violence and asylum

3.1. Introduction

There is a growing amount of evidence demonstrating that a significant number of LGBT persons in Council of Europe member states experience physical violence, harassment or assault because of their real or perceived sexual orientation and gender identity. Such violence may take different forms but is often driven by deep hatred, intolerance, disapproval or rejection of the sexual orientation or gender identity of the person. A commonly used term in this regard is "hate crime" or "hate-motivated violence", which may be fuelled by speech and public expressions which spread, incite, promote or justify hatred, discrimination or hostility towards LGBT people. Such speech can be expressed by fellow citizens, but also by political and religious leaders or other opinion makers, whether circulated by the press or the Internet. Sometimes state actors are involved in violence or harassment against LGBT persons, and in some instances family members.

Violence against LGBT persons is often not recognised and frequently ignored as a problem. The majority of member states of the Council of Europe have no explicit legal basis which recognises sexual orientation and gender identity in hate crime legislation. The Committee of Ministers has emphasised the need for effective protection from hate crimes and other hate-motivated incidents.[124]

When violence or cumulative harassment, assault or other forms of harm reach a particular severity and threshold, LGBT persons may decide to flee their home town or even their country. There are many countries outside Europe where LGBT persons face serious human rights violations and persecution, including those due to criminalisation of consensual same-sex acts. In approximately 76 countries worldwide laws are in force which prohibit consensual same-sex sexual acts between adults.[125] In seven countries the death penalty is applied to homosexuals (Iran, Mauritania, Nigeria, Saudi Arabia, Sudan, United Arab Emirates and Yemen). In this regard, a joint statement was delivered in December 2008 at the United Nations General Assembly condemning killings, torture and arbitrary arrests of LGBT persons and other human rights violations.[126] The statement was supported by 67 states, including 41 member states of the Council of Europe. Some 85 states sponsored a similar statement in March 2011 at the UN Human Rights Council, among which were 43 Council of Europe member states.[127]

---

124. Committee of Ministers Recommendation CM/Rec(2010)5 on measures to combat discrimination on grounds of sexual orientation or gender identity, adopted on 31 March 2010, paragraphs 1-5.
125. ILGA, "State-Sponsored Homophobia: A World Survey of Laws Prohibiting Same-Sex Activity Between Consenting Adults", May 2010, p. 4.
126. General Assembly, Sixty-third session, Agenda item 64(b), 22 December 2008, A/63/635, Promotion and protection of human rights: human rights questions, including alternative approaches for improving the effective enjoyment of human rights and fundamental freedoms.
127. United Nations, Human Rights Council, 16th session, Agenda item 8, 22 March 2011, Follow-up and implementation of the Vienna Declaration and Program of Action.

3.2. Violence against LGBT persons

Hate-motivated violence and hate crimes against LGBT persons take place in all Council of Europe member states.[128] Expert reports conclude that "homophobic hate crimes and incidents often show a high degree of cruelty and brutality. ... They are also very likely to result in death. Transgender people seem to be even more vulnerable within this category."[129] Such attacks often occur in public places and include attacks on LGBT venues, such as attacks on gay discos or on the premises of LGBT organisations. Attacks may also happen in the street when gay, bisexual or lesbian couples simply hold hands as a sign of affection for each other. Attacks which result in death, or outright murders, are not uncommon either.

National legislation in Council of Europe member states

The incitement of hatred, violence or discrimination on grounds of sexual orientation is considered as a criminal offence in only 18 member states (Andorra, Belgium, Croatia, Denmark, Estonia, France, Iceland, Ireland, Lithuania, Monaco, the Netherlands, Norway, Portugal, Romania, Slovenia, Spain, Sweden and the United Kingdom[130]). Similarly, homophobic intent is accepted as an aggravating factor in common crimes in only 14 member states: Andorra, Belgium, Croatia, Denmark, France, Greece, Lithuania, the Netherlands, Portugal, Romania, Slovenia, Spain, Sweden and the United Kingdom. In only two member states is gender identity or transphobic hate crime explicitly addressed in hate crime legislation (see Map 3.1).[131]

In the remaining member states sexual orientation and/or homophobic motivation are neither a criminal offence nor an aggravating factor. However, several of these states have provisions in the criminal law that could include hate crime or hate speech against LGBT persons under definitions such as "other population group" or "any social group".[132]

---

128. Poelman M. and Smits D., "Agressie tegen holebi's in Brussel-Stad", Apeldoorn, Antwerp, 2007; Tiby E., "Hatbrott? Homosexuella kvinnor och mäns berättelser om utsatthet för brott", Stockholms universitet Kriminologiska institutionen, 1999; MANEO – the gay Anti-Violence-Project in Berlin; Buijs L., Duyvendak J. W. and Hekma G., "Als ze maar van me afblijven", Amsterdam School for Social Science Research, Amsterdam, 2008; Abramowicz M. (ed.), "Situation of bisexual and homosexual persons in Poland", Kampania Przeciw Homofobii and Lambda Warsaw, 2007.
129. OSCE/ODIHR, "Hate Crimes in the OSCE Region – Incidents and Responses. Annual report for 2006", OSCE/ODIHR, Warsaw, 2007, p. 53.
130. England and Wales have a specific incitement criminal offence on grounds of sexual orientation and gender identity. They also have a homophobic intent statutory aggravation. Scotland has no specific incitement criminal offence on grounds of sexual orientation or gender identity but has both homophobic and transphobic statutory aggravations for common crime.
131. This overview is based on European Union Agency for Fundamental Rights, "Homophobia, Transphobia and Discrimination on Grounds of Sexual Orientation and Gender Identity: 2010 Update – Comparative Legal Analysis", 2010; OSCE/ODIHR, "Hate Crimes in the OSCE Region – Incidents and Responses. Annual Report for 2009", Warsaw, 2010; national contributions (legal reports).
132. However, in four countries, provisions in the criminal law against incitement to hatred cannot be extended to LGBT persons as they are restricted to predefined groups only (Austria, Bulgaria, Italy and Malta). Source: European Union Agency for Fundamental Rights, "Homophobia, Transphobia and Discrimination on Grounds of Sexual Orientation and Gender Identity: 2010 Update – Comparative Legal Analysis", 2010, pp. 42-43.

Regarding gender identity only Sweden and part of the United Kingdom (Scotland) explicitly address gender identity, gender expression or transphobic hate crime or hate speech in the criminal law. In a few member states the prohibition of incitement to hatred, discrimination or violence on the ground of "sex" or "gender" may include violence against transgender persons. Transphobic hate crime or hate speech may also be considered to be categorised under the heading of homophobia, but this is not clear from the national legislative frameworks.

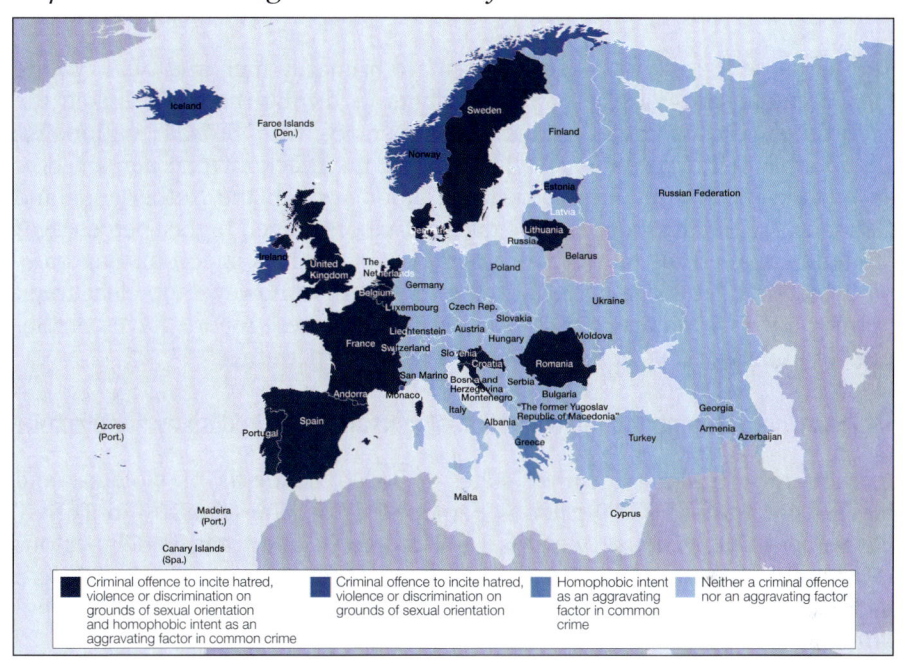

Map 3.1: Hate crime legislation inclusive of sexual orientation

Perpetrators of violence against LGBT persons

Visibility of LGBT persons in the public space is a common predictor for homophobic and transphobic attacks to take place – the more visible LGBT persons are, and the more they are recognised or perceived as LGBT, the more they run the risk of being exposed to aggression. Transgender persons may be attacked due to their physical appearance, which may not fully correspond to the gender in which they are living, making them more visible and thus a potential object for ridicule, hatred and the like. Research conducted for this report points to the fact that LGBT persons, to a large extent, conceal their identity in public settings throughout the member states in order to avoid possible violent reactions. A study in Slovenia found that "gays and lesbians resort to mimicry to adjust to the heteronormativity of public spaces. They outwardly redefine their partnership and re-contextualise it as 'just a friendship'. Only in circumstances that appear sufficiently safe do some allow the expression of intimacies that point to their sexual status. Gays and lesbians are, as a rule, aware of the environment in general and the heteronormativity determining this environment."[133]

Perpetrators of violent attacks against LGBT persons do so because of their rejection of what they label as "visible" homosexuality or transgressing traditional gender roles. It is important to note that violence also happens against persons who are perceived to be LGBT even when they are not. The perpetrators are often unknown to the victim, though in some cases relatives or colleagues are the perpetrators. Lesbian women are more likely to be assaulted by older perpetrators, often acting on their own, and often by somebody they know. In some instances, for example LGBT sex workers, the client could be the perpetrator.

The perpetrators of anti-LGBT violence are primarily men and often young men in organised groups. Several interlocutors during the study linked the occurrence of hate crime against LGBT persons with broader nationalist, xenophobic or racist tendencies in society who attack anyone perceived as an outsider.[134] In a few member states, among which the Netherlands and Germany, some public debate has taken place on alleged higher percentages of members of ethnic minority or migrant communities in committing hate-motivated incidents against LGBT persons. There is, however, no clear trend in this direction and research is scarce. However, these reports have contributed to understanding some of the motives of perpetrators.[135]

Violence, harassment and the collection of sensitive private data by state actors

Interlocutors in some member states reported incidents of violence and harassment against LGBT persons perpetrated by state actors.[136] In Turkey harassment and violence towards LGB and especially transgender persons in Istanbul, Ankara, Mersin and Eskisehir was flagged as a major concern by several interlocutors, including in a report published by the Istanbul Provincial Human Rights Board.[137]

---

133. Švab A. and Kuhar R., *The Unbearable Comfort of Privacy: Everyday Life of Gays and Lesbians*, Politike: Ljubljana, 2005, pp. 95-96, also quoted in European Union Agency for Fundamental Rights (FRA), "Homophobia and Discrimination on Grounds of Sexual Orientation and Gender Identity in the European Union Member States: Part II – The Social Situation", 2009, p. 35.
134. European Union Agency for Fundamental Rights, "Homophobia and Discrimination on Grounds of Sexual Orientation and Gender Identity in the EU Member States: Part II – The Social Situation", 2009, p. 42; National contribution (sociological report) on Serbia, p. 7; National contribution (sociological report) on Russian Federation, pp. 25-26.
135. For example Buijs L., Duyvendak, J. W. and Hekma G., "Als ze maar van me afblijven", Amsterdam: Universiteit van Amsterdam, Amsterdam School for Social Science Research, 2008.
136. FRA national contribution (sociological report) on Greece, pp. 5, 11 and FRA national contribution (legal report) on Greece pp. 28-30; FRA national contribution (sociological report) on Romania, p. 5; national contribution (sociological report) on Albania, p. 8; national contribution (sociological report) on Armenia, pp. 3, 9-11; national contribution (sociological report) on Georgia, pp. 8-10; national contribution (sociological report) on "the former Yugoslav Republic of Macedonia", pp. 8-9; national contribution (sociological report) on Moldova, pp. 8, 12-13; national contribution (sociological report) on Serbia, pp. 9-10; national contribution (sociological report) on Turkey, pp. 7, 9-12; national contribution (sociological report) on Ukraine, p. 16.
137. Report of TC Istanbul Valiliği, Sayı B054VLK4340300/521/3764; National contribution (sociological report) on Turkey, p. 11; Human Rights Watch, "We Need a Law for Liberation" – Gender, Sexuality, and Human Rights in Changing Turkey", May 2008, p. 75.

In some member states NGOs reported that law-enforcement agencies have kept records on a person's sexual orientation. For example, in Austria and the United Kingdom police have kept databases of gay and bisexual men who were convicted in the past for consensual, although then illegal, same-sex acts. These records are still visible on criminal records and may show up, for example when employers check the credentials of job applicants. Whereas in the United Kingdom this has led to the introduction of legislation remedying this situation[138] some Austrian citizens have filed complaints at the European Court of Human Rights.[139]

In Ukraine, NGO reports document experiences of Ukrainian gay men who were arrested in a park late at night, subsequently photographed by police and had their fingerprints taken.[140] In a pending case before the European Court of Human Rights an applicant from Romania claims he has been detained, questioned, photographed and fingerprinted because of his homosexuality.[141] Again in Ukraine, during the investigation of a criminal case connected with the murder of a gay man, NGO reports refer to the police raiding the gay club "Androgin" in Kiev during the night of 10 to 11 April 2009. Over 80 people were allegedly detained and taken to a police station. Some people reported rude and abusive treatment by police officers and also claimed that the officers used force against them. At the police station, the officers took fingerprints and photos of those detained.[142] These reports come six years after the Parliamentary Assembly of the Council of Europe invited the Ukrainian authorities "to investigate allegations of police harassment of the lesbian and gay community and to take disciplinary action as appropriate".[143]

In Azerbaijan during 2009 police raided bars which LGBT persons visit and arrested almost 50 people. Police reportedly held the individuals and threatened to expose their sexual orientation publicly unless they paid a bribe.[144] A film documentary from Azerbaijan in which several people testify about their experiences also points to such incidents of blackmail.[145]

UN treaty bodies and UN special rapporteurs have, in relation to Azerbaijan, the Russian Federation and Turkey, urged these states to end acts of violence

---

138. The UK Government has introduced the Protection of Freedoms Bill which, among other issues, will expunge convictions for now-legal consensual same-sex sex from criminal records.
139. European Court of Human Rights, *F.J. v. Austria*, Application No. 2362/08, case pending; *E.B. v. Austria*, Application No. 26271/08, case pending; *H.G. v. Austria*, Application No. 48098/07, case pending.
140. Nash Mir, "Overview of LGBT human rights situation in Ukraine in 2010", Kiev, Ukraine, p. 5.
141. European Court of Human Rights, *Adrian Costin Georgescu v. Romania*, Application No. 4867/03, case pending.
142. Ukraine national contribution (legal report) p. 40.
143. Resolution 1346 (2003), Honouring of obligations and commitments by Ukraine, adopted by the Assembly on 29 September 2003 (27th Sitting), paragraph 8, iii.
144. US Bureau of Democracy, Human Rights, and Labor, US Department of State "Human Rights Report: Azerbaijan", 2009, section 1, paragraph c.
145. ILGA-Europe and COC Netherlands, "Everyone has the right to life, liberty and security of person". Documentary.

and harassment by the police against LGBT persons.[146] In some instances LGBT human rights defenders have been a target of such harassment and violence. The UN Special Representative on the situation of human rights defenders pointed out in 2007 that "In numerous cases ... police or government officials are the alleged perpetrators of violence and threats against defenders of LGBTI rights. In several of these cases ... police officers have, allegedly, beaten up or even sexually abused these defenders of LGBTI rights." The Special Representative reminded states of their responsibility for protecting defenders against violence and threats.[147]

Violence in the family

While many LGBT persons meet acceptance and respect in the family, many others may have to hide their sexual orientation from family members because they are afraid of bad repercussions. Systematically collected data on the scale of the problem are unavailable, but NGOs report the following: in France, 16% of LGBT persons reported they had been beaten at home by homophobic family members.[148] Homophobic violence in the family was also reported by lesbian and bisexual women in, among others, Georgia[149] and Azerbaijan.[150] Transgender people in Moldova reported[151] beatings from their fathers in an attempt to "cure" them and similar reports came from other countries. A survey in Scotland (United Kingdom) found 73% of the respondents experiencing at least one type of transphobic emotionally abusive behaviour from a partner or ex-partner; 47% of respondents had experienced some form of sexual abuse from a partner or ex-partner; 17% threatening behaviour; 11% physical violence; and 4% sexual abuse.[152] An NGO report on Azerbaijan in 2009 stated that the "most frank displays of violence against lesbian and bisexual women occur in the home, and include verbal and physical abuse, confinement indoors, compulsion, compulsory marriage" as well as the threat of crimes to avenge family honour.[153] The prevalence of domestic violence against LGBT persons is difficult to assess, but LGBT NGOs described family pressure, harassment, control and, in some cases, violence as invisible or under-reported. More research is needed to identify the level of violence or

---

146. See Concluding Observations on Azerbaijan, CCPR/C/AZE/CO/3, 13 August 2009, paragraph 19; Report of the Special Representative of the Secretary-General on the situation of human rights defenders, Addendum: Summary of cases transmitted to Governments and replies received, A/HRC/10/12/ADD.1, 4 March 2009, paragraphs 2574-2577 (Turkey); Concluding Observations on Russian Federation, CCPR/C/RUS/CO/6, 29 October 2009, paragraph 27.
147. Report of the Special Representative of the Secretary-General on the situation of human rights defenders, A/HRC/4/37, 24 January 2007, paragraph 96.
148. National contribution (sociological report) on France, p. 6.
149. National contribution (sociological report) on Georgia, p. 11.
150. "The Violations of the Rights of Lesbian, Gay, Bisexual, Transgender Persons in Azerbaijan – A Shadow Report", submitted to the UN Human Rights Committee, July 2009, p. 13.
151. National contribution (sociological report) on Moldova, p. 14.
152. Roch A., Ritchie G. and Morton J., "Out of Sight, Out of Mind? Transgender People's Experience of Domestic Abuse", Scotland: LGBT Youth Scotland, Equality Network, 2010, p. 5.
153. "The Violations of the Rights of Lesbian, Gay, Bisexual, Transgender Persons in Azerbaijan – A Shadow Report", submitted to the UN Human Rights Committee, July 2009, p. 13.

rejection LGBT people experience in their families. A positive r
opment in this regard is the adopted Council of Europe Co
preventing and combating violence against women and domesti(
it will also apply to lesbian, bisexual and transgender women.[154]

Hate speech

Speech which is likely to incite, spread or promote hatred against LGBT persons may create a climate where hate-motivated violence against them becomes an accepted phenomenon. While Article 10 of the European Convention on Human Rights guarantees the freedom of expression, this right is not absolute. Restrictions are permitted on speech or other expressions which incite to xenophobia, anti-Semitism and the like[155] as such speech is incompatible with the values proclaimed and guaranteed by the Convention. Two Committee of Ministers' recommendations[156] as well as the Council of Europe's White Paper on Intercultural Dialogue[157] call on the member states to take steps to combat speech which are likely to produce the effect of inciting, spreading or promoting hatred or discrimination. In Recommendation CM/Rec(2010)5, the Committee of Ministers points to the fact that a "specific responsibility is vested with the public authorities and officials to refrain from statements that may be understood as legitimising hatred or discrimination and to promote tolerance and respect for their human rights".[158] The Commissioner for Human Rights has publicly spoken out against hate speech on numerous occasions.[159]

During the research for this report numerous examples of often strong hate expressions were identified in Council of Europe member states. For example in relation to attempts to organise a Pride march in the Russian Federation a regional governor was quoted as saying: "Tolerance?! Like Hell! Faggots should be torn apart. And their pieces should be thrown in the wind."[160] In 2009, when organisers of a Gay Pride event in Serbia held a press conference, protestors outside were reportedly shouting: "Faggots, we will kill you."[161] In Bosnia and

---

154. The convention was opened for signature in Istanbul on 11 May 2011.
155. See, for example, European Court of Human Rights, *Incal v. Turkey*, Application No. 22678/93, judgment of 8 June 1998.
156. Committee of Ministers Recommendation No. R (97) 20 on "hate speech", adopted on 30 October 1997; Committee of Ministers Recommendation CM/Rec(2010)5 on measures to combat discrimination on grounds of sexual orientation or gender identity, paragraphs 6-8.
157. The Council of Europe White Paper on Intercultural Dialogue "Living Together As Equals in Dignity", section 5.1, 2008.
158. Committee of Ministers Recommendation CM/Rec(2010)5 on measures to combat discrimination on grounds of sexual orientation or gender identity, paragraphs 6-8.
159. Viewpoint, "Homophobic policies are slow to disappear", 16 May 2007; Viewpoint, "Gay Pride marches should be allowed – and protected", 24 July 2006.
160. Statement of Mr Betin, Governor of the Tambov Region, as quoted in ILGA-Europe, "Human Rights + Responsibility + Respect. A contribution to the Council of Europe conference: Human Rights in Culturally Diverse Societies: challenges and perspectives", p. 3; GayRussia.ru, 29 July 2008, "Activists intend to take the case to courts up to Strasbourg".
161. Human Rights Watch, Letter to the President of the Republic of Serbia, 16 November 2009.

Herzegovina, a YouTube clip was posted representing a direct death threat to one of the organisers of the Queer Sarajevo Festival in 2008, depicting her being beheaded. The latter situation led the Special Rapporteur on the Situation of Human Rights Defenders, together with the Special Rapporteur on the Promotion and Protection of the Right to Freedom of Opinion and Expression, to send a communication to the Bosnian authorities.[162] A communication was also sent by the Special Rapporteur to the Bulgarian authorities on 27 June 2008 regarding a Gay Pride Parade scheduled to take place in Sofia the day after, expressing her serious concerns for "speech which may incite hatred".[163] Other examples of web-based hate groups were reported from Latvia and Portugal. [164]

The European Court of Human Rights has shown little tolerance for hate statements, in particular when they are used by authorities as an argument for defending a ban on a Gay Pride march. In the landmark case *Alekseyev v. Russia*[165] the Court stated:

> *As regards any statements calling for violence and inciting offences against the participants in a public event, such as those by a Muslim cleric from Nizhniy Novgorod, who reportedly said that homosexuals must be stoned to death ..., as well as any isolated incidents of threats of violence being put into practice, they could have adequately been dealt with through the prosecution of those responsible. However, it does not appear that the authorities in the present case reacted to the cleric's call for violence in any other way than banning the event he condemned. By relying on such blatantly unlawful calls as grounds for the ban, the authorities effectively endorsed the intentions of persons and organisations that clearly and deliberately intended to disrupt a peaceful demonstration in breach of the law and public order.*[166]

Data on violence against LGBT persons

Official data on the scale and nature of police violence against LGBT persons and family violence is scarce. Official data on hate crimes and hate incidents are also scarce but data collected and published annually by the OSCE/ODIHR show that 15 Council of Europe member states collect data on crimes committed against LGBT persons (Andorra, Belgium, Croatia, Cyprus, France, Germany, Iceland, Ireland, Liechtenstein, the Netherlands, Norway, Serbia, Spain, Sweden and the United Kingdom).[167] However, not all these 15 member

---

162. Communication by the Special Rapporteur on the Situation of Human Rights Defenders and the Special Rapporteur on the Promotion and Protection of the Right to Freedom of Opinion and Expression, 27 November 2008, referred to in *Sexual Orientation and Gender Identity in Human Rights Law: Reference to Jurisprudence and Doctrine of the United Nations Human Rights System*, 2010, p. 38.
163. Ibid., p. 39.
164. The Latvian NoPride Association and the Portuguese Partido Nacional Renovador.
165. European Court of Human Rights, *Alekseyev v. Russia*, Applications Nos. 4916/07, 25924/08 and 14599/09, judgment of 21 October 2010.
166. Ibid., paragraph 76.
167. OSCE/ODIHR, "Hate Crimes in the OSCE Region – Incidents and Responses. Annual Report for 2009", Warsaw, 2010, pp. 18, 77-81.

states actually provided data to ODIHR. In fact only four states (Germany, Norway, Sweden and the United Kingdom) submitted data on homophobic hate crimes to ODIHR and only two of those states, Sweden and the United Kingdom, submitted data figures on hate crimes committed against transgender persons. Some other member states provided information on incidents but did not have comprehensive data sets. Yet other member states, such as Finland, do collect data on hate crime but do not necessarily disaggregate according to the motive or target group,[168] which makes it hard to get a complete overview of the scale of homophobic and transphobic hate crimes and hate incidents.

It can be observed that the United Kingdom has the most comprehensive data collection system on hate crimes.[169] In 2007, 988 criminal court cases were initiated against suspects of LGBT hate crimes; 759 persons were convicted, while in 2009 these figures had risen to 1 078 and 868 respectively.[170] Norway reported that in 2009 it recorded 36 crimes committed against LGBT persons based on bias motivation.[171] Germany reported that in 2009 it recorded 164 crimes motivated by a bias against sexual orientation, 45 of which were violent crimes.[172] In Sweden, in 2008, 1 055 hate crimes against LGB persons were recorded in Sweden of which 1 046 had a homophobic motive. In the same year 14 crimes were recorded against transgender persons.[173] In 2009, Sweden recorded 1 060 hate crimes against LGB persons of which 1 040 were homophobic crimes. In the same year the police recorded 30 hate crimes targeting transgender persons.[174] Public authorities in Turkey counted seven murdered transgender persons in 2008 and 2009.[175]

One should, however, keep in mind that these figures cannot be easily compared. As the OSCE/ODIHR observes: "there is still a paucity of clear, reliable and detailed data on the nature and scope of hate crimes in the OSCE area. … Even where statistics exist, they are not always disaggregated according to bias motivation, type of crime or outcome of prosecution. … Since different participating States keep statistics in different manners, it is also not possible to make comparative judgments on the extent of hate crimes."[176] Indeed,

---

168. FRA national contribution (legal report) on Finland, p. 10.
169. OSCE/ODIHR, "Hate Crimes in the OSCE Region – Incidents and Responses. Annual Report for 2007", Warsaw, 2008.
170. FRA national contribution (legal report) for the United Kingdom, p. 100.
171. OSCE/ODIHR, "Hate Crimes in the OSCE Region – Incidents and Responses. Annual Report for 2009", Warsaw, 2010, p. 79.
172. Ibid., p. 78.
173. OSCE/ODIHR, "Hate Crimes in the OSCE Region – Incidents and Responses. Annual Report for 2008", Warsaw, 2009, p. 56.
174. OSCE/ODIHR, "Hate Crimes in the OSCE Region – Incidents and Responses. Annual Report for 2009", Warsaw, 2010, p. 80.
175. Information provided by the Turkish authorities to the Office of the Commissioner for Human Rights. Three convictions were found by the courts.
176. OSCE/ODIHR, "Hate Crimes in the OSCE Region – Incidents and Responses. Annual Report for 2009", Warsaw, 2010, p.14.

some data refer to the number of court cases initiated, other data refer to the number of persons convicted, and yet other data refer to hate crimes or hate incidents recorded or police reports registered.

In addition to the data provided by member states additional information for this report has been identified in studies carried out by NGOs or expertise centres.[177] These studies argue that hate crimes and hate-motivated incidents against LGBT persons are experienced by significant numbers of people. ILGA-Europe lists examples of hate killings against LGBT persons in the period 2005-2008 in the Netherlands, Portugal, the Russian Federation, Turkey and the United Kingdom.[178] The Transgender Murder Monitoring Project of Transgender Europe recorded 36 hate killings in Council of Europe member states in the period 2008 to November 2010:[179] Italy and Turkey (thirteen cases each), Spain (three cases), Germany and the United Kingdom (two cases each), Albania, Portugal and Serbia (one case each). Most of these victims were transgender women, and a significant number of them worked as irregular migrants in the adult entertainment industry. In a 2008 report by London's Metropolitan Police[180] 65% of lesbian and transgender women surveyed experienced incidents that they considered as homophobic or transphobic in nature. Nearly two thirds (64%) of the women having experienced such incidents said they had a short-term or long-term impact on them. Of the incidents mentioned by these women, 83% went unreported to the police. Other studies in the United Kingdom[181] provide similar accounts of experiences of harassment, physical or sexual abuse. In Sweden, a third of the transgender respondents in a survey reported that they had been the victim of violence, abuse or harassment at some point in their lives.[182]

Obstacles in understanding data on hate crime

There are several obstacles regarding data on hate crime against LGBT persons: first of all, the lack of a legal basis recognising sexual orientation and gender identity in hate crime legislation in a majority of member states. As the previous section described, only less than half of the member states have relevant criminal law provisions. Regarding gender identity, the lack of recognition of gender identity in hate crime legislation is even more worrisome.

A second obstacle is the low number of victims who report a hate-motivated incident or a hate crime to the police. According to an NGO study in Poland,

---

177. For example "Geweld tegen homoseksuele mannen en lesbische vrouwen. Een literatuuronderzoek naar praktijk en bestrijding". Movisie, Netherlands, 2009.
178. Submission to the Council of Europe Expert Committee: ILGA-Europe, "The Preparation of a Recommendation on Discrimination Based on Sexual Orientation and Gender Identity", February 2009, paragraph 57-59.
179. Transgender Europe, Trans Murder Monitoring project.
180. Metropolitan Police, "Women's Experience of Homophobia and Transphobia: Survey Report", London, 2008, p. 16.
181. Dick S., "Homophobic Hate Crime – The Gay British Crime Survey 2008", Stonewall, 2008, p. 3; Turner L., Whittle S. and Combs R., "Transphobic Hate Crime in the European Union", Press for Change, London, 2009, p. 18.
182. Statens Folkhälsoinstitut, "Homosexuellas, bisexuellas och transpersoners hälsosituation, Återrapportering av regeringsuppdrag att undersöka och analysera hälsosituationen bland hbt-personer", FHI, Östersund, 2005, pp 41, 68.

15% of hate incidents against LGBT persons are reported.[183] In the United Kingdom this figure is 23% according to a NGO survey.[184] Research confirms that many victims of a hate crime do not report this because of fear of exposure of their sexual orientation or gender identity or because of a lack of trust in the judiciary.[185] Others are reluctant to go to the police because they have previously encountered police officers being reluctant to believe in the existence of a homophobic motive for a crime or incident. In France, Greece, Hungary and Italy, more than half of the transgender respondents in a NGO hate crimes study were not confident of the police.[186] Inactivity by the police in reply to transgender persons' calls has also been reported, for example in Croatia.[187]

Anonymous reporting schemes have been initiated in the Netherlands, Denmark and Slovenia in an attempt to get a more realistic view of the scale of the problem.[188] Hate incidents and hate crimes can be reported anonymously on the Internet. Another tool is the "third party reporting system", where victims or witnesses of hate crime can report the incidents online or by phone. Examples of such initiatives were identified in France, Germany and the United Kingdom.

A third obstacle is the lack of skills and awareness as well as concrete tools among law-enforcement agencies to register cases of hate crime. The element of hatred is not always recognised by the police when a victim reports the incident. Hate crimes may be seen as an act of "hooliganism" or bodily injury. If not registered by the police as such, the hate motivation is likely not to be considered as an aggravating factor during the investigation with the result that the homophobic or transphobic motive becomes indistinguishable during the prosecution of hate crime cases. For example, a study in Sweden[189] and a NGO report on Turkey[190] show that the bias motivation is sometimes not taken into account in the trial and sentencing. However, regarding Turkey, in 2007 a court recognised for the first time an element of hate motivation and elements of prejudice in a relevant case.[191] In another case in 2009 a Turkish

---

183. Abramowicz M. (ed.), "Situation of bisexual and homosexual persons in Poland", Kampania Przeciw Homofobii & Lambda Warsaw, 2007, p. 15.
184. Dick S., "Homophobic Hate Crime – The Gay British Crime Survey 2008", Stonewall, 2008.
185. European Union Agency for Fundamental Rights, "Homophobia and Discrimination on Grounds of Sexual Orientation and Gender Identity in the EU Member States: Part II – The Social Situation", 2009, pp. 43-45; national contribution (sociological report) on Armenia, p. 11; national contribution (sociological report) on Croatia, p. 9; national contribution (sociological report) on Georgia, p. 11; national contribution (sociological report) on Moldova, pp. 11-12; national contribution (sociological report) on Serbia, p. 10.
186. Turner L., Whittle S. and Combs R., "Transphobic Hate Crime in the European Union", Press for Change, London, 2009, p. 55.
187. National contribution (legal report) on Croatia, p. 20.
188. Quoted in European Union Agency for Fundamental Human Rights, "Homophobia and Discrimination on Grounds of Sexual Orientation and Gender Identity in the European Union Member States: Part II – The Social Situation", 2009, p. 43.
189. Tiby E., "En studie av homofoba hatbrott i Sverige", Forum för levande historia, Stockholm, 2006, p. 11.
190. Human Rights Watch, "We need a Law for Liberation, Gender, Sexuality and Human Rights in a Changing Turkey", 2008, pp. 24, 47.
191. Ankara 11th High Criminal Court, case number: 2007/250, decision number: 2008/246.

court acknowledged that the perpetrator committed the crime with a homophobic or transphobic motivation.[192] It should be recalled that the European Court of Human Rights has held that there is a positive obligation under the Convention for authorities to take all reasonable steps to uncover and establish any bias motive in a crime as part of an effective investigation[193] and to investigate and punish bias-motivated criminal acts.

The OSCE/ODIHR designed the former Law Enforcement Officer Programme (LEOP) on combating hate crime, which has been piloted in Spain and Hungary, fully implemented in Croatia and in the process of full implementation in Poland and Bosnia and Herzegovina. The newly revised programme, Training Against Hate Crime for Law Enforcement (TAHCLE), is pending implementation in Bulgaria, pursuant to a signed agreement. A pilot project in nine European countries (Denmark, France, Germany, Ireland, Latvia, Portugal, Romania, Sweden and the United Kingdom) has been set up to focus on how the police handle hate crime cases. The project has developed a toolkit for handling hate crimes, including a database for reporting, a website with information about hate crime, training material for police and information material for LGBT people.[194]

3.3. Asylum on the grounds of sexual orientation and gender identity

Violence and hatred directed at LGBT persons may be of such severity and/or framed by an absence of state protection that LGBT persons see no other solution than to flee their country of origin. While most LGBT asylum seekers in Council of Europe member states come from outside the Council of Europe geographical area, there have also been incidental reports of refugees who have fled from one Council of Europe member state to another.[195] While international and European human rights standards have been adopted in this field, this chapter demonstrates that the implementation of these standards still faces serious obstacles.

International standards

When the situation in the home country amounts to a risk for LGBT persons to be subjected to persecution, including torture or other cruel, inhuman or degrading treatment or punishment, they have the right to seek and enjoy

---

192. Ankara 6th High Criminal Court, decision of 15 October 2009.
193. These are positive obligations flowing from Articles 2 and 3 of the European Convention on Human Rights read in conjunction with Article 14. European Court of Human Rights, *Cobzaru v. Romania*, Application No. 48254/99, judgment of 26 July 2007; *Secic v. Croatia*, Application No. 40116/02, judgment of 31 May 2007, and *Angelova and Iliev v. Bulgaria*, Application No. 55523/00, judgment of 26 July 2007.
194. The project website for Tracing and Tackling Hate Crimes against LGBT Persons: www.stophatecrime.eu.
195. For example, a refugee from the Russian Federation (Ingushetia) was granted asylum in Poland in 2007 on the ground of her sexual orientation (FRA national contribution (legal report) on Poland, p. 30). Another refugee from the same region was granted asylum in 2006 in France. In 2006 a citizen from Bosnia and Herzegovina was granted subsidiary protection in France (FRA national contribution (legal report) on France, p. 28).

asylum in another country. This is enshrined in Article 14 of the Universal Declaration of Human Rights and further elaborated in the 1951 Convention Relating to the Status of Refugees[196] (hereafter the 1951 Convention) and its Protocol of 1967.[197] States Parties to the 1951 Convention are prohibited from expelling or returning a refugee to a country (*non-refoulement*) where his or her life or freedom would be threatened. This is an obligation to ensure that asylum seekers are not returned or sent to a country where their life is threatened or where they face the risk of torture, inhuman or degrading treatment or punishment. Complementary to refugee status is the subsidiary protection in situations where the individual does not fulfil the requirements for obtaining refugee status but is in need of international protection. Subsidiary protection may be invoked notably on grounds relating to the rights and freedoms contained in the UN Convention against Torture and other Cruel Inhuman or Degrading Treatment, the UN Covenant on Civil and Political Rights or the European Convention on Human Rights.

Member states of the Council of Europe also have the positive obligation under the European Convention on Human Rights to provide protection in order to guarantee the right to life (Article 2) and to prohibit torture, inhuman or degrading treatment or punishment (Article 3). Protection against *refoulement* is further granted under the ground of Article 3 of the European Convention on Human Rights, which thus goes beyond the mere scope of the 1951 Convention. As a well-established principle, the prohibition of torture and inhuman or degrading treatment or punishment, includes an obligation for contracting states not to expel a person to a country where there are substantial grounds to believe that that person will face a real risk of being subjected to treatment contrary to Article 3.[198] Two cases in this regard are pending before the European Court of Human Rights.[199] They involve a lesbian woman from Zimbabwe and a homosexual man from Iran who fear that they run the risk of being subjected to ill-treatment if returned to their countries of origin.

The Committee of Ministers stressed the need for the member states bound by the 1951 Convention[200] to recognise that a well-founded fear of persecu-

---

196. United Nations, Convention relating to the Status of Refugees, adopted on 28 July 1951 by the United Nations Conference of Plenipotentiaries on the Status of Refugees and Stateless Persons convened under General Assembly Resolution 429(V) of 14 December 1950.
197. United Nations, Protocol relating to the Status of Refugees, 606 U.N.T.S. 267, entered into force 4 October 1967. Of the 47 member states of the Council of Europe, 44 are parties to both the 1951 Convention and to the 1967 Protocol. Andorra and San Marino are not parties to the Convention and Monaco is party to the 1951 Convention only.
198. European Court of Human Rights, *Soering v. United Kingdom*, Application No. 14038/88, judgment of 7 July 1989, Series A No. 161, p. 35, paragraph 88, and *Chahal v. United Kingdom*, Application No. 22414/93, judgment of 15 November 1996, paragraph 74.
199. European Court of Human Rights, *D. B. N. v. United Kingdom*, No. 26550/10, case pending; European Court of Human Rights, *K. N. v. France*, No. 47129/09, case pending.
200. United Nations, Convention relating to the Status of Refugees, adopted on 28 July 1951 by the United Nations Conference of Plenipotentiaries on the Status of Refugees and Stateless Persons convened under General Assembly Resolution 429(V) of 14 December 1950.

tion based on sexual orientation or gender identity may be a valid ground for granting refugee status and asylum.

Finally, for European Union Member States, Council Directive 2004/83/EC of 29 April 2004 on minimum standards for the qualification and status of third country nationals or stateless persons as refugees or as persons who otherwise need international protection and the content of the protection granted (hereafter the Qualification Directive)[201] applies. This directive defines a "refugee" following the wording of the 1951 Convention, and provides for subsidiary protection.[202] The formulation "member of a particular social group" is spelled out in Article 10(1)(d) and explicitly mentions sexual orientation.[203] Gender identity is not referred to in the Qualification Directive but may be included under the ground of "membership of a particular social group", especially in light of the wording in Article 10(1)(d), which refers to "gender-related aspects".

The UN Special Rapporteur on Torture and Other Forms of Cruel, Inhuman or Degrading Treatment or Punishment[204] and the UN Committee Against Torture[205] have expressed concerns regarding the situation of LGBT asylum seekers. The UNHCR has released a Guidance Note on Refugee Claims Relating to Sexual Orientation or Gender Identity, which recognises that LGBT persons may fall within the refugee definition of the 1951 Convention if they have a well-founded fear of persecution, including serious abuse, discrimination and criminalisation.[206] Whether or not a fear of persecution is well founded should be assessed by authorities taking into account the statements of the claimant in the context of background information concerning the situation in the country of origin.[207] The concept of persecution involves serious human rights violations, including a threat to life or freedom, as well as other serious harm. A pattern of harassment and discrimination could, on cumulative grounds, also reach the threshold of persecution.[208] While sexual orientation or gender identity are not explicitly addressed in the list of grounds of the 1951 Convention, the UNHCR Guidance Note maintains that these two grounds may be subsumed under the grounds of "political opinion", "religion" or "membership of a particular social group".[209] For the purposes of granting refugee status to LGBT asylum

---

201. Council Directive 2004/83/EC of 29 April 2004.
202. Cf. Article 2(e) and Article 15.
203. Cf. Article 10(1)(d).
204. UN General Assembly, UN Doc. A/59/324, 1 September 2004, paragraph 39.
205. UN Committee against Torture, General Comment No. 2 on implementation of Article 2 by states parties, 2007, paragraph 21.
206. UNHCR, Guidance Note on Refugee Claims Relating to Sexual Orientation or Gender Identity, 21 November 2008, paragraph 3.
207. UNHCR, "Handbook on Procedures and Criteria for Determining Refugee Status under the 1951 Convention and the 1967 Protocol relating to the Status of Refugees" (paragraphs 42-43), HCR/IP/4/Eng/REV.1. Reedited, Geneva, January 1992.
208. UNHCR, "Guidance Note on Refugee Claims Relating to Sexual Orientation or Gender Identity", 21 November 2008, paragraph 10.
209. Ibid., paragraphs 29-32.

seekers, it is particularly the ground of "membership of a particular social group" that is increasingly applied in cases.[210]

National legislation and data on LGBT asylum and refugee cases

Twenty-six member states have explicitly recognised in their national legislation that sexual orientation is included in the notion of "membership of a particular social group" (Austria, Belgium, Bulgaria, Croatia, Cyprus, the Czech Republic, Finland, France, Germany, Hungary, Iceland, Ireland, Italy, Latvia, Lithuania, Luxembourg, Malta, Moldova, the Netherlands, Poland, Portugal, Romania, Slovakia, Slovenia, Spain and Sweden). In the other member states there is no explicit mention in their legislation. There are, however, at least seven other member states which, even in the absence of such explicit recognition, have had asylum claims in which sexual orientation has been recognised as a ground for persecution (Denmark, Greece Norway, Switzerland, Turkey, Ukraine and the United Kingdom) evidenced by decisions of national competent bodies in these countries. In the other 12 member states which are parties to the 1951 Convention there is no explicit recognition of persecution on the basis of sexual orientation as a valid ground for asylum claims either in legislation or in actual successful cases filed by LGBT asylum seekers (Albania, Armenia, Azerbaijan, Bosnia and Herzegovina, Estonia, Georgia, Liechtenstein, Monaco, Montenegro, the Russian Federation, Serbia and "the former Yugoslav Republic of Macedonia").

Explicit recognition in national legislation of gender identity as a notion of "membership of a social group" is hard to find. The only member state explicitly mentioning gender identity as being encompassed in the notion of "membership of a particular social group" in its national asylum legislation is Iceland.[211] Moreover, transgender persons have been granted asylum in a few other member states, including in Austria, Belgium, Cyprus, the Netherlands and Switzerland.[212]

Regarding data collection, in two member states (Belgium and Norway) official statistics are collected in relation to LGBT asylum seekers. In Belgium[213] 116 cases were handled in 2006 of which 33 people were granted refugee status. For 2007 these figures were 188 (60 people granted refugee status) and in 2008 the figure increased to 226 (96 were granted refugee status or subsidiary protection). In 2009 the figure further increased to 362 (with 129 persons granted refugee or subsidiary protection status) and in 2010 the number of 522 was reached, out of which 156 received refugee protection.

---

210. Cf. UNHCR, "Guidelines on International Protection No. 2: 'Membership of a Particular Social Group' Within the Context of Article 1A(2) of the 1951 Convention and/or its 1967 Protocol Relating to the Status of Refugees" (HCR/GIP/02/02), 7 May 2002, paragraph 1.
211. National contribution (legal report) on Iceland, p. 5.
212. See for example (FRA) national contributions (legal reports) on Cyprus (p. 15) and Switzerland (pp. 17-18).
213. Information provided by the Commisariat Général aux Réfugiés et aux Apatrides (CGRS). The figures cover sexual orientation and gender identity asylum cases, but do not distinguish between the two.

In Norway, partial statistics suggest that in 2008-2009 11 people had claimed asylum on grounds of sexual orientation; a tentative overview from 2002 suggests that approximately 41 cases involved individuals seeking asylum for persecution or ill-treatment due to their sexual orientation.[214] In the other member states no official statistics are available. However, some member states provided estimates on the number of applications on the grounds of sexual orientation and gender identity. The Swedish Migration Board estimated in 2002 the number of applicants seeking asylum in Sweden on grounds of sexual orientation or gender identity to be approximately 300 per year.[215] In the Netherlands the applications of homosexual and transgender asylum seekers amount to approximately 200 per year.[216] In Italy, according to the Ministry of Internal Affairs, in the period from 2005 to the beginning of 2008, at least 54 cases were filed, of which at least 29 were granted refugee status or humanitarian protection.[217]

Challenges and obstacles in and during the asylum procedure

LGBT asylum seekers are confronted with particular obstacles in making their claim and difficulties are faced by authorities in assessing asylum claims on the grounds of sexual orientation or gender identity.[218]

First, criminalisation of consensual same-sex relations in the countries of origin of the applicants is interpreted and evaluated differently by the competent bodies in Council of Europe member states. The nature of the legislation and its potential impact on the safety and life of the applicant are evaluated in terms of a certain degree of gravity that the persecution has to attain in order to be considered as threatening to the asylum seeker. UNHCR has noted in this respect: "Criminal laws prohibiting same-sex consensual relations between adults have been found to be discriminatory and to constitute a violation of the right to privacy. The very existence of such laws, irrespective of whether they are enforced and the severity of penalties they impose, may have far-reaching effects on LGBT persons' enjoyment of their fundamental rights."[219]

---

214. UNHCR, "Fleeing for Love: Asylum Seekers and Sexual Orientation in Scandinavia", Research Paper No. 181, 2009, p. 4.
215. European Union Agency for Fundamental Rights, "Homophobia, Transphobia and Discrimination on Grounds of Sexual Orientation and Gender Identity: 2010 Update – Comparative Legal Analysis", 2010, p. 60.
216. IND Informatie- en Analysecentrum, "Evaluatie Gendergerelateerd Vreemdelingenbeleid in Nederland", The Hague, Ministry of Justice, 2008.
217. FRA national contribution (legal report) on Italy, p. 15.
218. See, for example, UNHCR Expert Roundtable, *Summary Conclusions: Asylum-Seekers and Refugees Seeking Protection on Account of their Sexual Orientation and Gender Identity*, November 2010; UNHCR Discussion Paper, *The Protection of Lesbian, Gay, Bisexual, Transgender and Intersex Asylum-Seekers and Refugees*, 22 September 2010; Human Rights First: "Persistent Needs and Gaps: The Protection of Lesbian, Gay, Bisexual, Transgender and Intersex (LGBTI) Refugees: An Overview of UNHCR's Response to LGBTI Refugees and Recommendations to Enhance Protection", 2010, pp. 8-9.
219. UNHCR, "UNHCR Guidance Note on Refugee Claims Relating to Sexual Orientation and Gender Identity", 2008, p. 10.

Decisions in asylum cases in the member states illustrate the different approaches to this end. In some member states the existence of criminal provisions prohibiting "homosexual conduct" in itself is not sufficient to justify the granting of refugee status. Examples of this line of thinking imply that applicants can avoid persecution in the country of origin by living discreetly, meaning to conceal their sexual orientation. UNHCR raised in this regard that Norwegian immigration authorities generally consider that LGBT persons must be required to keep their sexual orientation or gender identity hidden from their local community if spreading this knowledge could lead to persecution.[220] It is of particular concern that in such case law there is an attempt to make distinctions between a mere "tendency" to be gay or lesbian, which the individual could hide or conceal, and "irreversible" homosexuality, which would lead to recognising the individual concerned as deserving of international protection.

In other member states, for example Belgium, the Netherlands and Sweden, the competent authorities have recognised the right of lesbian and gay refugees to live openly in their countries of origin. These countries have removed the inconsistency between asylum claims based on sexual orientation, and those based on other grounds, as members of ethnic or religious minorities, and political dissidents are also not expected to hide their ethnicity, religion, or political beliefs. A ruling in the United Kingdom in 2010 also reached such a conclusion, stressing that "to reject his application on the ground that he could avoid the persecution by living discreetly would be to defeat the very right which the [1951] Convention exists to protect – his right to live freely and openly as a gay man without fear of persecution".[221] In yet other member states, for example Germany,[222] different courts have adopted both positions. The German judiciary has in the context of this "discretion requirement" referred questions for a preliminary ruling concerning homosexual asylum seekers to the Court of Justice of the European Union to get clear guidance to the question whether a homosexual person can be expected to live with his or her sexual orientation in his or her home country in secret.[223]

A second obstacle is the assessment of the credibility of the asylum seeker, as LGBT asylum cases build on intimate private life issues. Under the threat of criminal laws, family or community violence, internalised homophobia, fear of dismissal from employment or discrimination LGBT asylum seekers may have concealed their sexual orientation or gender identity in the country of origin and may have no "proof" of their sexual orientation or gender identity.

---

220. UNHCR, "Fleeing for Love: Asylum Seekers and Sexual Orientation in Scandinavia", Research Paper No. 181, 2009, p. 13.
221. *H. J. (Iran) and H. T. (Cameroon) v. Secretary of State for the Home Department*, UKSC 31, 7 July 2010, UK Supreme Court, paragraph 82.
222. FRA national contribution (legal report) on Germany, pp. 20-23.
223. Court of Justice of the European Union, C-563/10, *Kashayar Khavand v. Federal Republic of Germany*, case pending.

UNHCR has noted: "Self-identification as LGBT should be taken as an indication of the individual's sexual orientation. While some applicants will be able to provide proof of their LGBT status, for instance through witness statements, photographs or other documentary evidence, they do not need to document activities in the country of origin indicating their different sexual orientation or gender identity."[224] There are several accounts where asylum officers do not accept the asylum claims based on sexual orientation for example because an applicant is married in a heterosexual relationship or has children. How the applicant should "prove" his or her sexual orientation and/or gender identity has also been the subject of several court cases.[225] A Swedish study on asylum procedures finds that "distrust is often based on stereotypical preconceptions of sexual orientation and gender expression",[226] and in Denmark similar conclusions were reached.[227] Phallometric testing has been used in several cases in the Czech Republic in order to "test" whether the applicants were gay or not.[228] The use of such tests, and their results, can infringe a person's right to be free from inhuman or degrading treatment under Article 3 of the European Convention on Human Rights, as was also acknowledged in a decision by a regional administrative court in Germany[229] ordering the stay of transfer under the Dublin II Regulation of an Iranian gay man because of the possible use of 'phallometry' in the Czech Republic. There is a strong need for using sensitive interview techniques and sensitisation of asylum officers in line with UNHCR guidelines.[230]

Third, LGBT asylum seekers in asylum centres face difficulties when their sexual orientation or gender identity is known. The reactions of other asylum seekers, especially if they come from the same region, could include harassment and ostracism among others. In some instances staff remedied the situation.[231] In others, asylum seekers are afraid to stay in the centres because of

---

224. Ibid., p. 15.
225. For example, *R v. Secretary of State for the Home Department ex parte Vraciu* (1995) Appeal No. HX/70517/94; *J v. Secretary of State for the Home Department* [2006] EWCA Civ 1238.
226. Borg H., Törner E. and Wolf-Watz O., "Norm-Critical Study of the Swedish Asylum Examination, produced for the Swedish Migration Board by Ramböll Management Consulting", 2010, p. 4.
227. The Danish Refugee Appeals Board, "Formandskabet 13. Beretning 2004", 2004, p. 146.
228. European Union Agency for Fundamental Rights, "Homophobia, Transphobia and Discrimination on Grounds of Sexual Orientation and Gender Identity: 2010 Update – Comparative Legal Analysis", 2010, pp. 58-59; "Testing Sexual Orientation: A Scientific and Legal Analysis of Plethysmography in Asylum and Refugee Status Proceedings", ORAM, 2010.
229. Schleswig-Holsteinisches Verwaltungsgericht, 6 B 32/09, 7 September 2009.
230. UNHCR, "Guidelines on International Protection No. 1: "Gender-Related Persecution Within the Context of Article 1A(2) of the 1951 Convention and/or its 1967 Protocol relating to the Status of Refugees", HCR/GIP/02/01, 7 May 2002.
231. European Union Agency for Fundamental Rights, "Homophobia and Discrimination on Grounds of Sexual Orientation and Gender Identity in the EU Member States: Part II – The Social Situation", 2009, p. 101; European Union Agency for Fundamental Rights, "Homophobia, Transphobia and Discrimination on Grounds of Sexual Orientation and Gender Identity: 2010 Update – Comparative Legal Analysis", 2010, pp. 58-60; National contribution (legal report) on Switzerland, p. 17.

the risk of abuse,[232] marginalisation and harassment from other applicants. Another specific problem for transgender persons is access to trans-specific health care while being in an asylum centre or in the asylum procedure. There may not be any possibility of accessing hormonal treatment or other therapy. This may lead to grave health problems as interrupting hormonal treatment is detrimental for their health, which will put a further burden on a person already traumatised.

---

232. UNHCR, "Fleeing for Love: Asylum Seekers and Sexual Orientation in Scandinavia". Research Paper No. 181, 2009, p. 19; Helsinki Citizen's Assembly – Turkey and ORAM – Organisation for Refuge, Asylum and Migration, "Unsafe Haven: The Security Challenges Facing Lesbian, Gay, Bisexual, and Transgender Asylum Seekers and Refugees in Turkey", 2009.

4. Participation: freedoms of assembly, expression and association

4.1. Introduction

Freedom of association, freedom of expression and freedom of assembly are three basic human rights which are essential for a full and active participation in society. Indeed, hindrances to the free enjoyment of these rights impinge on the possibility of individually or collectively participating in civil, social and political life. These freedoms are pivotal to combating discrimination, to enhance communication, to favour dialogue and to improve civil society's understanding of issues pertaining to the human rights of LGBT persons.

The enjoyment of the rights to associate, express and assemble by LGBT persons and their organisations is guaranteed in most of the member states of the Council of Europe. However, as this report has demonstrated, public representation and visibility of LGBT persons may be received with hostile reactions, denial or rejection. In a few Council of Europe member states this has led to restrictions to the freedoms of expression, assembly and association of LGBT persons. Such cases have included the impossibility to organise Pride parades and cultural festivals, the denial of registering LGBT associations, and refusal or obstacles when publishing and distributing material on issues concerning sexual orientation and gender identity.

4.2. International and European standards

International human rights standards guarantee the respect of these three freedoms irrespective of a person's sexual orientation or gender identity. LGBT persons are free to express their views, organise assemblies and register organisations which focus on issues concerning sexual orientation and/or gender identity. The freedom of expression is protected in Article 19 of the Universal Declaration of Human Rights as well as in Article 19 of the International Covenant on Civil and Political Rights. The European Convention on Human Rights ensures the protection of the right to freedom of expression in Article 10 and the European Union Charter for Fundamental Rights enshrines it in Article 11. Freedom of association and assembly are protected in Article 20 of the Universal Declaration of Human Rights and in Articles 21 and 22 of the International Covenant for Civil and Political Rights. Provisions guaranteeing these freedoms are also found in other international instruments.[233] In Europe the right to freedom of assembly and association is enshrined in the European Convention on Human Rights (Article 11) and in the European Union Charter for Fundamental Rights (Article 12). The Committee of Ministers in its recommendation called for

---

233. Such as the Convention on the Elimination of All Forms of Racial Discrimination or the Convention on the Rights of the Child.

measures to be adopted in order to ensure the effective enjoyment of these rights irrespective of one's sexual orientation or gender identity.[234]

The rights to associate, express and assemble are not absolute. In some instances legitimate limitations can be applied by authorities. However, according to the European Convention on Human Rights, restrictions should be (1) prescribed by law, (2) have a legitimate aim, and (3) be necessary in a democratic society to achieve those aims. When applicants bring a case to the European Court of Human Rights, the Court will therefore verify whether there is an interference by public authorities and then apply this three-part test.

Legitimate aims for restricting freedom of expression, assembly and association include, in particular, national security, public safety, prevention of disorder or crime, protection of health or morals and protection of the rights and freedoms of others.

The European Court of Human Rights has further clarified to what extent limiting these three freedoms is in compliance with the European Convention on Human Rights. The Court has stressed that when evaluating a specific restriction applied in a national context it is faced "not with a choice between two conflicting principles, but with a principle of freedom of expression that is subject to a number of exceptions which must be narrowly interpreted".[235] Regarding the possibility of invoking the "morality" justification for limitations to the freedom of expression the Court has maintained that, in order to promote pluralism, broadmindedness and openness in society, it is necessary also to accept opinions, expressions and information that may be welcomed unfavourably by a part of the population.[236] The authorities should not therefore limit freedom of expression on the basis of their moral outlook, but rather be obliged to ensure freedom of expression even if the matters expressed are controversial. This has also been stated in a case of freedom of expression of LGBT persons, in the judgment of *Alekseyev v. Russia*.[237] In relation to freedom of assembly the Court has held,[238] and later restated in both *Bączkowski and Others v. Poland*[239] and *Alekseyev v. Russia*,[240] that protection of freedom of assembly goes as far as also including those assemblies that are not positively perceived by the majority. There is

---

234. Committee of Ministers Recommendation CM/Rec(2010)5 on measures to combat discrimination on grounds of sexual orientation or gender identity, adopted on 31 March 2010, paragraphs 9 and 13.
235. European Court of Human Rights, *The Sunday Times v. United Kingdom*, Application No. 13166/87, judgment of 26 April 1979, paragraph 65.
236. European Court of Human Rights, *Handyside v. United Kingdom*, Application No. 5493/72, judgment of 7 December 1976, paragraph 49.
237. European Court of Human Rights, *Alekseyev v. Russia*, Applications Nos. 4916/07, 25924/08 and 14599/09, judgment of 21 October 2010.
238. European Court of Human Rights, *Stankov and the United Macedonian Organisation Illinden v. Bulgaria*, Applications Nos. 29221/95 and 29225/95, judgment of 2 October 2007, paragraph 77.
239. European Court of Human Rights, *Bączkowski and Others v. Poland*, Application No. 1543/06, judgment of 3 May 2007.
240. European Court of Human Rights, *Alekseyev v. Russia*, Applications Nos. 4916/07, 25924/08 and 14599/09, judgment of 21 October 2010.

also a positive obligation for the authorities to protect the participants of an assembly from violent counter-demonstrators.[241]

4.3. Situation in the member states

Freedom of assembly

LGBT persons and their organisations in many member states of the Council of Europe have been invisible from public life for a long time. The "Stonewall Riots" of June 1969 in New York, during which LGBT persons protested against continuing harassment by the police, marked a turning point for the freedom of expression, assembly and association of LGBT persons. The events of June 1969 constituted an important inspiration for LGBT human rights defenders to stand up publicly and to denounce the discriminations they experienced. LGBT Pride events have since 1969 been celebrated in many places around the world. Over time, other specific events have also become recurring, such as the Transgender Day of Remembrance celebrated annually on 20 November to commemorate victims of transphobic violence.

The enjoyment of the right to freedom of assembly is sometimes considered as a litmus test for the attitudes of society towards LGBT persons. In most member states Pride parades and similar cultural events take place without significant problems and participants enjoy police protection if need be. Political parties and commercial companies may participate in Pride events. Trade unions in at least nine member states (France, Germany, Ireland, Italy, the Netherlands, Portugal, Spain, Sweden and the United Kingdom) have also participated in Pride festivals.

However, in some member states bans or administrative impediments have been imposed or the police have not effectively protected participants from violent counter-demonstrators. Opposition to events promoting the human rights of LGBT persons have their roots in sensitivity of parts of the population, as such events raise public attention to issues of discrimination based on sexual orientation and gender identity. The mere visibility of LGBT persons at such events is seen as provocative by a majority of the population, as evidenced by surveys carried out, for instance, in Serbia,[242] where 73% of those surveyed said they oppose public demonstrations of LGBT persons.

Since 2004 in at least 12 member states there have been cases of bans and/or administrative impediments on Pride events or other large public cultural LGBT events (Bulgaria, Estonia, Latvia, Lithuania, Moldova, Poland, Romania, the Russian Federation, Serbia, Turkey, Ukraine and "the former Yugoslav Republic of Macedonia"). In eight other member states (Albania, Armenia,

---

241. European Court of Human Rights, *Plattform "Ärtze für das Leben"*, Application No. 10126/82, judgment of 21 June 1988, paragraphs 32 and 34.
242. Gay Straight Alliance, "Prejudices Exposed – Homophobia in Serbia". Public opinion research report on LGBT population, 2008, February-March 2008, p. 6.

Azerbaijan, Cyprus, Georgia, Monaco, Montenegro and San Marino), no large public cultural or Pride events have ever been organised, while in the remaining 27 member states no significant problems have been encountered (see Map 4.1) even though in some of them, bans of Pride events have been called for.

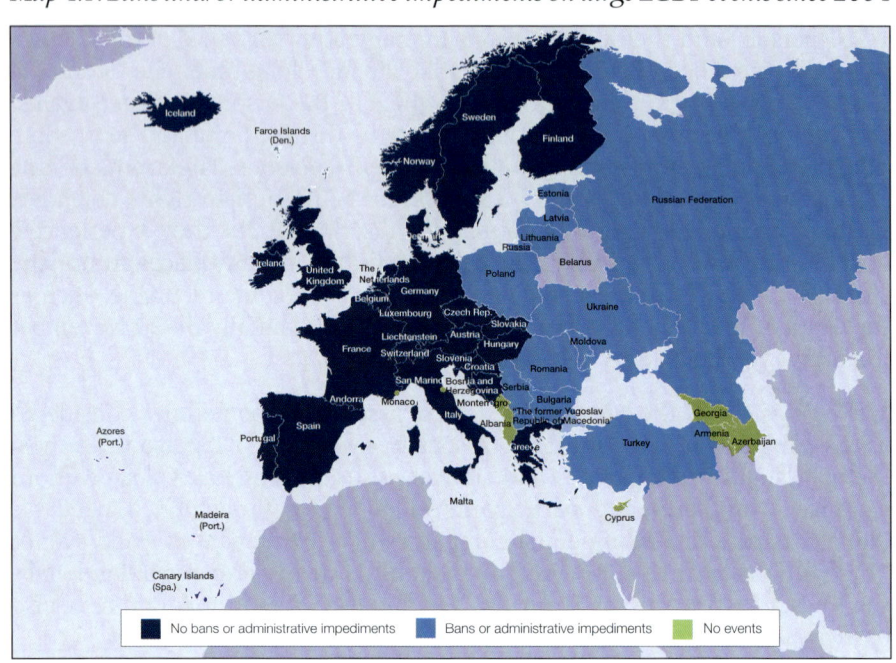

Map 4.1: Bans and/or administrative impediments on large LGBT events since 2004

Bans of Pride parades and other LGBT cultural events have since 2004 occurred in a handful of member states, notably the Pride parades in Latvia (in 2005 and 2006), Lithuania (in 2007 and 2008), in Romania (in 2005) and in "the former Yugoslav Republic of Macedonia" (in 2007, when an LGBT event in Skopje was denied authorisation). In the Russian Federation, since 2005 notifications by the NGO GayRussia to hold a Pride parade in the city have been turned down by the Municipality of Moscow every year. However, activists have organised events, despite the impossibility of holding a Pride parade, which resulted in incidents and attacks from homophobic groups and which lacked effective protection of participants by the authorities.[243] In a recent European Court of Human Rights ruling[244] the Court found a violation of the Convention because it did not accept the argument from the authorities that the possibility of violent counter-demonstrations is a valid justification to

---

243. Human Rights Watch and ILGA-Europe, "We have an upper hand! – Freedom of Assembly in Russia and the Human Rights of Lesbian, Gay, Bisexual and Transgender People", June 2007.
244. European Court of Human Rights, *Alekseyev v. Russia*, Applications Nos. 4916/07, 25924/08 and 14599/09, judgment of 21 October 2010.

prevent the Pride parade from taking place.[245] The Court recalled its previous case law that there is a positive obligation by states to protect the participants from violent counter-demonstrations.

As for administrative impediments, the landmark case *Bączkowski and Others v. Poland* concerned a request from the authorities to present a traffic plan to the organisers of the 2005 Pride parade in Warsaw, resulting in an impingement on the right to freedom of assembly, as ascertained by the European Court of Human Rights.[246] Administrative impediments have also been used in other member states in order to deny authorisation to hold Pride parades. Administrative impediments have been justified by authorities on the ground that the police would not be able to protect the participants from hostile or violent counter-demonstrations. This has been the case in, amongst others, Estonia, Latvia, Moldova, the Russian Federation, Serbia, Turkey and Ukraine. In some instances, such as in Serbia and Moldova, the authorities made the location of the event conditional for police protection. Sometimes they would propose locations which were far away from the city centre.

Counter-demonstrations as a reaction to Pride parades are not uncommon in member states and may be held by religious communities, nationalist or extreme right-wing groups. While most of these counter-demonstrations are carried out within the limits of the right to freedom of assembly, others take the form of organised attacks on participants in Pride parades, resulting in clashes and incidents. This has been the case in at least 15 member states since 2004 (Bosnia and Herzegovina, Bulgaria, Croatia, the Czech Republic, Estonia, Hungary, Italy, Latvia, Moldova, Poland, Romania, the Russian Federation, Serbia, Sweden and Ukraine[247]). Sometimes counter-reactions have had a wider reach and have been promoted and sustained by political or religious figures. European institutions, including the Commissioner for Human Rights, have expressed concern for violence and limitations on the right to freedom of assembly of LGBT persons.[248] Violent clashes seriously hamper the possibility for LGBT persons to peacefully demonstrate for their human rights and contribute to fostering hostility and prejudices. The OSCE has developed a set of guidelines to provide guidance to states on how to respect the freedom of assembly.[249] The guidelines contain a principle of non-discrimination on the part of the authorities in guaranteeing the exercise of the right to freedom of assembly, including on the ground of sexual orientation, while they do not make mention of gender identity.

---

245. Ibid., paragraph 51.
246. European Court of Human Rights, *Bączkowski and Others v. Poland*, Application No. 1543/06, judgment of 3 May 2007.
247. See (FRA) national contributions.
248. Commissioner for Human Rights, "Pride events are still hindered – this violates freedom of assembly", 2010, Human Rights Comment.
249. OSCE/ODIHR, "Guidelines on Freedom of Peaceful Assembly" (2nd edn), Warsaw, 2010.

Freedom of expression

Interference in the exercise of freedom of expression of LGBT persons is not frequent in Council of Europe member states. If it happens, it is usually directed at impeding expressions, opinions and information concerning sexual orientation or gender identity from being circulated because of possible negative reception by the majority population.

On the most basic level the freedom of expression of LGBT persons can be restricted when the legislator drafts bills in order to impose sanctions on those accused of "promoting homosexuality". This has been the case in three member states since 2004. In Lithuania the Law on the Protection of Minors against the Detrimental Effects of Public Information was passed in December 2009. According to that law, information deemed to be detrimental to minors includes information promoting sexual relations, expressing contempt for family values and encouraging the concept of entry into marriages and families other than by the definition of marriage in the Lithuanian Constitution as being exclusively between a man and a woman.[250] The first version of the law, which was passed in July 2009, included "promotion of homosexual, bisexual and polygamous relationships". Following national and international criticisms this reference was dropped but the law still contains the expression "contempt for family values", the scope of which remains unclear.[251] Moreover, drafts to supplement the Penal Code and the Code of Administrative Offences have been proposed, which aim to prevent issues of homosexuality from being raised in public. Adoption of these proposals is still pending but they would be likely to include, if adopted, a limitation to the right to freedom of expression of LGBT persons. In Poland in 2007, the attempt to adopt a similar law was not successful and the amendments to the Law on Education System, proposed by the then Minister of Education, were rejected.[252]

In the Russian Federation in 2003 and in 2006 two federal bills punishing the so-called "propaganda of homosexuality" were proposed in the Duma. Such "propaganda" would include any public statement, including in the mass media, and public displays of a "homosexual lifestyle". The draft bills formulated as punishment "deprivation of the right to occupy certain posts or practise certain activities for a period of two to five years".[253] The Supreme Court of the Russian Federation, however, maintained when reviewing the draft bill of 2006 that:

---

250. FRA national contribution (legal report) on Lithuania, pp. 45-46; European Union Agency for Fundamental Rights, "Homophobia, Transphobia and Discrimination on Grounds of Sexual Orientation and Gender Identity: 2010 Update – Comparative Legal Analysis", 2010, pp. 34-35.
251. FRA national contribution (legal report) on Lithuania, pp. 45-46.
252. FRA national contribution (legal report) on Poland, pp. 67-68.
253. Federal Law on Amending the Criminal Code of the Russian Federation to Criminalise the Propaganda of Homosexuality, Draft No. 367150-3: proposed by Deputy of the State Duma A. V. Chuyev on 15 September 2003; Federal Law on Amending the Criminal Code of the Russian Federation to Criminalise the Propaganda of Homosexuality, Draft No. 311625-4: proposed by deputy of the State Duma A. V. Chuyev on 20 June 2006.

in accordance with the current legislation sodomy and lesbianism are considered as criminal only if these deeds are associated with the violence or with the threat of it, or in taking advantage of the victim's helpless condition. Committing the mentioned deeds by mutual consent do not form any crime or administrative offence. The Federal Law on the Mass Media prohibits the distribution of information that promotes pornography, and a cult of violence and cruelty, but does not exclude the possibility of releasing erotic publications under certain conditions (Articles 3 and 37).[254]

The drafts were not supported by the government and were also rejected by the state Duma.

Despite the fact that such law initiatives failed on the federal level, in the region of Ryazan a Regional Law on Administrative Offences punishing the "Propaganda of Homosexuality" among minors[255] was adopted in 2008, together with a Regional Law on the Protection of Morality and Health of Minors, which contains similar provisions.[256] In 2009 Russian LGBT activists appealed to the Constitutional Court of the Russian Federation, and asked the Constitutional Court to test the constitutionality of the Regional Law of Ryazan. The Constitutional Court in 2010 refused to consider the complaint regarding this law, and noted that "the family, motherhood and childhood in the traditional interpretation, received from our ancestors, are the values that provide a continuous change of generations, and are conditions for the preservation and development of the multinational people of the Russian Federation, and therefore require a special state protection".[257]

Interference with the freedom of expression can also take the form of explicit bans on specific materials or performances in which LGBT issues are presented or discussed. Although not common in most member states, incidents have been registered in three member states and concerned diverse kinds of publications. In Poland in 2006 the publication of *Compass*, the manual for human rights education of the Council of Europe, constituted the reason for the then Polish government to dismiss the director of the government agency which had financed and distributed the Polish version of the manual. In the view of the government the manual did not reflect Polish values since it did not depict homosexuality as a deviation.[258] The

---

254. On the Draft Federal Law on Amending the Criminal Code of the Russian Federation to Criminalise the Propaganda of Homosexuality: Official Response of the Supreme Court of the Russian Federation No. 492-2/общ. of 20 April 2006.
255. Law of Ryazan Region on Administrative Offences: passed by the Ryazan Region Duma on 24 November 2008.
256. Law of Ryazan Region on the Protection of Morality and Health of Children in Ryazan Region: passed by the Ryazan Region Duma on 22 March 2006.
257. On refusal to consider the complaint of citizens Alekseyev Nikolay Aleksandrovich, Baev Nikolay Viktorovich and Fedotova Irina Borisovna regarding the violation of their constitutional rights by Article 4 of the Law of Ryazan Region on the Protection of Morality and Health of Children in Ryazan Region: Decision of the Constitutional Court of the Russian Federation of 19 January 2010.
258. FRA national contribution (legal report) on Poland, p. 67.

Secretary General of the Council of Europe[259] and the Commissioner for Human Rights spoke publicly against this point of view.[260]

In Turkey, following the decision of the Ankara Public Prosecutor Office to seize an LGBT magazine in 2006,[261] which was justified on the ground of Article 28 of the Turkish Constitution and the Law on Criminal Procedure, the NGO which had published the magazine filed an appeal. This appeal was unsuccessful and after the final decision of the Ankara Criminal Court of First Instance, the NGO brought the case before the European Court of Human Rights,[262] which is now pending. In Azerbaijan the novel "Artush and Zaur", by the author Alekper Aliyev, portraying the love between an Azerbaijani man and an Armenian man, was removed by the police from a big bookstore in Baku.[263]

Freedom of association

LGBT NGOs have been formed in nearly all member states. LGBT NGOs in some member states of the Council of Europe face challenges on the most basic level: to register their organisation and statutes. Restrictions on the freedom of association have been observed in five member states during the period 2004-2010: Armenia, Azerbaijan, the Russian Federation, Turkey and Ukraine. Such restrictions by the authorities are usually motivated on the ground that the founding documents and scope of the association are contrary to national law. Authorities have also used the argument that the scope of the association is in contrast to or undermines national moral values. Furthermore, administrative issues may arise in relation to registration formalities.

In the Russian Federation, notwithstanding the constitutional guarantee of the freedom of association, some LGBT organisations have been refused registration. In February 2010, the Ministry of Justice of the Russian Federation denied state registration of the organisation "Marriage Equality Russia". The organisation, which included in its statutes that it wished to achieve marriage equality for LGBT people in the Russian Federation, was denied registration because its founding documents would be contrary to the legislation of the Russian Federation as well as incompatible with the Family Code of the Russian Federation, which defines marriage as a union between a man and a woman.[264] Another organisation, Rainbow House, was denied registration because the goals of the organisation aimed "to protect the rights and freedoms of individuals, including persons of non-traditional sexual orientation, to promote education of identity of these individuals as citizens of

---

259. Article by Terry Davis, Secretary General of the Council of Europe, published in *Gazeta Wyborcza* of 2 October 2006.
260. Commissioner for Human Rights, Memorandum to the Polish Government, 20 June 2007, CommDH(2007)13, paragraphs 53-55.
261. National contribution (legal report) on Turkey, p. 41.
262. European Court of Human Rights, *KAOS LG v. Turkey*, Communicated to the Government for observations, Application No. 4982/07, Date of Decision to Communicate 16 June 2009.
263. National contribution (legal report) on Azerbaijan, p. 6.
264. National contribution (legal report) on the Russian Federation, pp. 16-17.

society which are equal in rights and value". According to the authorities "the propaganda of non-traditional sexual orientation", which in turn "could lead to undermining the security of the Russian society and State", would "undermine the moral values of the society, and undermined the sovereignty and territorial integrity of Russia because of a reduction of the population", which means that the organisation would "infringe on institutions of family and marriage, protected by the State".[265] The decision was unsuccessfully challenged domestically by the NGO,[266] which therefore decided to file an application at the European Court of Human Rights.[267]

Other cases in the Russian Federation involved organisations in Arkhangelsk and St Petersburg. In the first case, the NGO Rakurs in Arkhangelsk had already been registered in 2007 as an NGO working on women's rights, but had at a later stage wished to change its statutes by defining its purposes as encompassing issues pertaining to homophobia, discrimination and support to LGBT persons. The refusal to accept the amendments to the statutes was motivated by the authorities with reference to the argument that they were in conflict with the Law on Countering Extremist Activity.[268] In the second case, the organisation Gender-L, which had organisational aims similar to those of the Rakurs organisation, successfully challenged in court the denial for registration. Indeed, there is evidence that more LGBT organisations have been able to register, such as two LGBT NGOs in St Petersburg and Murmansk whose statutes explicitly mention the fight against discrimination and homophobia as the purpose of the associations.

Problems with the registration of the statutes of LGBT associations have also been registered in Armenia, Azerbaijan and Ukraine. In Ukraine in 2008, despite the absence of formal limitations, the "People of Bukovina" NGO was requested to delete from its statute the wording "sexual orientation" and compelled to use "gender orientation".[269] Another Ukrainian organisation, the Lviv LGBT Organisation Total, reported similar problems. In Armenia, NGOs report being unable to include in their statutes references to LGBT issues, sexual orientation or gender identity, although the authorities have denied that this is the case.[270] In Azerbaijan the NGO Gender and Development managed to get the registration but reported that they were contacted several times during the registration process by the State Security Committee regarding the target groups, scope of the organisation and the organisation's relations with other countries.

---

265. National contribution (legal report) on the Russian Federation (Annex to Chapter 2, case 6).
266. On the cassation appeal of A. V. Zhdanov on the decision of Centralny District Court of Tyumen, case No. 33-2383.
267. European Court of Human Rights, *Aleksandr Zhdanov and Rainbow House v. Russia*, Application No. 12200/08.
268. Decision of the Office of the Ministry of Justice of the Russian Federation on the Arkhangelsk Region and Nenets Autonomous District of 31 May 2010 No. 03-09-3266 on the refusal of state registration of amendments to the constituent documents of a public association.
269. National contribution (legal report) on Ukraine, p. 14.
270. National contribution (sociological report) on Armenia, p. 8.

In Turkey, LGBT organisations have faced problems in relation to attempts by the authorities to close them down. There is a pattern in this regard and problems were reported in different cities, such as in Ankara (KAOS LG), Istanbul (Lambdaistanbul), Izmir (Black Pink Triangle) and in Bursa (Rainbow Association). Arguments used to carry out these operations, later successfully challenged in Turkish courts by the NGOs, related in all these cities to issues concerning the contrariety of the activities of these associations to Turkish moral and family values. The case of Lambdaistanbul was heard in 2009 by the Turkish Supreme Court of Appeals after the Istanbul 3rd Civil Court of First Instance had ruled for the closure of the association. The Supreme Court in deciding the case ascertained that the scope of activity of the association did not go against moral values and therefore overturned the previous decision.[271] However, although Lambdaistanbul defeated the legal challenge to its registration, the Supreme Court of Appeals left open the possibility of future challenges to freedom of association in its ruling: "The dissolution of the defendant organisation could still be demanded if it would act counter to its charter, in the ways of encouraging or provoking lesbian, gay, bisexual, transvestite and transsexual behaviour or acting with the aim of spreading such sexual orientations." Lambdaistanbul lodged a case challenging this aspect of the judgment at the European Court of Human Rights in June 2010.[272]

Restrictions to freedom of association are not exclusively limited to unlawful interference by the authorities in registration processes. They can also take the form of impediments for LGBT associations to carry out social and cultural activities in their premises or in locations rented out by private parties. Evidence for such occurrences were identified in, but not confined to, Bosnia and Herzegovina, Georgia, Italy, Lithuania, Serbia, Slovenia and the Russian Federation. Refusals to rent or to provide access to these locations are connected to the LGBT-related character of these events.

For instance, Organisation Q in Bosnia and Herzegovina was evicted from its premises by the landlord and the Lithuanian Gay League was unable to rent office space from another NGO working on disability issues.[273] In Slovenia the celebration of the 10th anniversary of the LGBT movement, to be held in a castle, was cancelled after the owner had discovered the nature of the event.[274] In the Russian Federation, the LGBT Film Festival "Side by Side" was prevented from taking place in 2007 because the owner of the premises intended to be used for the event in St Petersburg cancelled the booking, allegedly motivated in part by pressure from public authorities. A similar incident was also registered the following year when the owner of

---

271. Beyoğlu/Istanbul Civil Court of First Instance No. 3, Case No. 2009/65, Decision No. 2009/69. National contribution (legal report) on Turkey, pp 10-11.
272. European Court of Human Rights, *Lambda Istanbul v. Turkey*, Application No. 53804/10. The application has been registered but not yet communicated.
273. FRA national contribution (sociological report) on Lithuania, p. 13.
274. FRA national contribution (sociological report) on Slovenia, p. 6.

another facility in which the event was to take place cancelled the screenings following a threat to have the electricity cut off.[275] In Serbia the press conference of the Gay Straight Alliance was cancelled by the Director of the Sava Centar in Belgrade because it had been deemed inappropriate for the venue.[276] In Italy, LGBT associations in 2007 were prevented from taking part in the Conference for the Family organised by the Ministry of the Family and faced problems when seeking access to theatres and venues for organising public debates.[277]

---

275. National contribution (sociological report) on the Russian Federation, pp. 21-22.
276. National contribution (sociological report) on Serbia, p. 8.
277. National contribution (sociological report) on Italy, p. 7.

5. Privacy: gender recognition and family life

5.1. Introduction

Part of every life is private and member states have positive obligations under the European Convention on Human Rights to protect this private sphere. In fact, Article 8 on the right to respect for private and family life of the Convention has a vast scope of application. In addition to family life, it may also protect, for example, medical information, correspondence, collection of personal data and many issues related to self-identity. This chapter examines two aspects of private life which are particularly important for LGBT persons: the legal recognition of a person's preferred gender and family life in several respects.

First, gender or sex is an integral part of self-identity for practically all people, whether they are heterosexual, gay, lesbian or bisexual, and an especially intimate part of private life under Article 8 of the Convention. Gender identity is of course a crucial issue for transgender persons. People who are ill at ease with the gender they were assigned at birth may face difficulties in later life if they want to change their legal gender. This chapter starts with an analysis of the legislative framework and practice in place for the legal recognition of preferred gender and explores to what extent the authorities of member states protect transgender persons from interference with it.

Second, this chapter considers to what extent member states currently protect the private and family lives of LGBT persons and enable the respect due to them under Article 8. It starts with the ability to seal a legal partnership and examines whether same-sex couples receive the rights and benefits which are customarily granted to different-sex partners. Parental rights are of particular interest here because many LGBT persons have children and the rights to custody, inheritance and next-of-kin status need to be assured in the best interests of the child.

The European Court of Human Rights no longer considers that the right to marry under the European Convention of Human Rights must in all circumstances be limited to different-sex couples and has found it artificial to maintain that a same-sex couple cannot enjoy "family life" for the purposes of Article 8 of the Convention.[278] This landmark ruling from 2010 reflects a decade of rapid change that saw some Council of Europe member states introduce the right to marry for same-sex couples. However, Council of Europe member states are not obliged to give access to marriage to same-sex

---

278. *Schalk and Kopf v. Austria*, Application No. 30141/04, judgment of 24 June 2010, paragraph 55. It built on arguments in earlier cases, notably *Karner v. Austria*, Application No. 40016/98, judgment of 24 July 2003 and *Kozak v. Poland*, Application No. 13102/02, judgment of 2 March 2010, and was repeated in the case of *P. B. and J. S. v. Austria*, Application No. 18984/02, judgment of 22 July 2010. Until June 2010, the Court had interpreted Article 12 of the European Convention on Human Rights, which affords the right to marry and found a family to "men and women of marriageable age" as the prerogative of different-sex couples.

partners and they enjoy a wide margin of appreciation in this field under Article 12 of the Convention on the right to marry, which refers directly to national legislation. The Charter of Fundamental Rights of the European Union includes a gender-neutral Article 9 on the right to marry and found a family but recognises the subsidiarity principle vis-à-vis national legislation in this field. Yet member states that do not give cohabiting same-sex couples the opportunity to marry or enter into a legal partnership cannot treat such couples less favourably than cohabiting different-sex couples in the same situation, unless the less favourable treatment can be justified by very weighty reasons.

5.2. Recognition of transgender persons' new gender and name

European standards

For transgender persons it is crucial to acquire the state's legal recognition of the preferred gender. In practice this implies a rectification of the recorded sex on birth certificate or civil register. A second issue is the change of first name. Changes are also needed for other official documents such as passports, driving licences, social security or tax numbers as well as other documents including pension accounts, school diplomas, credit cards, or mortgage contracts. They may identify the bearer not only by name and gender explicitly, but also by an encoded "gender marker", such as 1 for men and 2 for women. For many transgender persons in Council of Europe member states these are complex and cumbersome processes.

The case law of the European Court of Human Rights has evolved over time and developed new standards on legal recognition of the preferred gender. In *Christine Goodwin v. United Kingdom*, in which the Court found a violation of Articles 8 and 12, the Court argued that there is "clear and uncontested evidence of a continuing trend in favour not only of increased social acceptance of transsexuals but of legal recognition of the new sexual identity of post-operative transsexuals".[279] Member states are therefore required to legally recognise the gender reassignment of these persons. This was reiterated in 2007 in the case of *L. v. Lithuania*, when the Court stressed that a legislative gap on full gender reassignment treatment left the applicant "in a situation of distressing uncertainty vis-à-vis his private life and the recognition of his true identity".[280]

---

279. European Court of Human Rights, *Christine Goodwin v. the United Kingdom*, Application No. 28957/95, judgment of 11 July 2002, paragraph 59. The Gender Recognition Act (2004) was enacted as a response to this judgment.
280. European Court of Human Rights, *L. v. Lithuania*, Application No. 27527/03, judgment of 11 September 2007, paragraph 59. The Committee of Ministers is supervising the execution of judgment in this case.

The Commissioner for Human Rights,[281] the Council of Europe's Committee of Ministers[282] and the Parliamentary Assembly[283] have also emphasised states' positive obligation in this regard. The Committee of Ministers has recommended member states to "take appropriate measures to make possible the change of name and gender in official documents in a quick, transparent and accessible way" as well as to "ensure, where appropriate, the corresponding recognition and changes by non-state actors with respect to key documents, such as educational or work certificates".[284]

The European Court gives states wide discretion for the means of recognising the preferred gender and name. In practice the requirements can be medical (for example surgery leading to sterilisation, a gender dysphoria diagnosis or a medical opinion, preceded by psychological or psychiatric treatment), legal (for example a court order, automatic divorce) or of another nature (for example being childless, "real-life experience" or the intention to live in the opposite gender for a specific period). In many member states there is a blurring of such legal and medical requirements. The length and cost of these procedures may vary significantly and result in them being beyond the reach of the interested parties. Procedures often involve fees for diagnosis, medical treatment and court proceedings, all of which can be a significant burden for a single individual.

To date, no cases have been judged by the European Court of Human Rights over requirements such as mandatory sterilisation and surgery leading to infertility. The Recommendation of the Committee of Ministers, however, states that requirements "including changes of a physical nature" should be regularly reviewed in order to remove abusive requirements.[285] Parliamentary Assembly Resolution 1728 (2010) calls upon member states to ensure that official documents reflect the individual's preferred gender identity, without any prior obligation to undergo sterilisation or other medical procedures such as sex reassignment surgery and hormonal therapy.[286]

National legislation regulating gender recognition

Twenty-four Council of Europe member states have adopted legislation on the legal recognition of the preferred gender. This is the case in Austria, Belgium, Cyprus, the Czech Republic, Denmark, Finland, Germany, Greece, Italy,

---

281. Commissioner for Human Rights, "Human Rights and Gender Identity", Issue Paper, Strasbourg, 2009.
282. Committee of Ministers Recommendation CM/Rec(2010)5 on measures to combat discrimination on grounds of sexual orientation or gender identity, adopted on 31 March 2010.
283. Council of Europe, Parliamentary Assembly Resolution 1728 (2010) on discrimination on the basis of sexual orientation and gender identity, adopted 29 April 2010.
284. Council of Europe, Recommendation CM/Rec(2010)5 of the Committee of Ministers on measures to combat discrimination against discrimination on grounds of sexual orientation or gender identity, paragraph 21.
285. Committee of Ministers Recommendation CM/Rec(2010)5 on measures to combat discrimination on grounds of sexual orientation or gender identity, adopted in 31 March 2010, paragraph 20.
286. Council of Europe, Parliamentary Assembly Resolution 1728 (2010) on discrimination on the basis of sexual orientation and gender identity, adopted 29 April 2010, paragraph 16.11.2.

Latvia,[287] Malta, Montenegro, the Netherlands, Norway, Portugal, Romania, the Russian Federation, Slovakia, Spain, Sweden, Switzerland (in some cantons only – no national legislation), Turkey, Ukraine and the United Kingdom.[288] In 10 Council of Europe member states this report has not identified legislation regulating the legal gender recognition. This is the case in Albania, Andorra, Armenia, Azerbaijan, Ireland,[289] Liechtenstein, Monaco, San Marino, Slovenia and "the former Yugoslav Republic of Macedonia". Nor did this study find evidence that these 10 states offer the possibility for transgender persons to have their preferred gender legally recognised in an alternative manner (in the absence of legislation). In 13 other member states transgender persons are able to have their new gender legally recognised, either through going to court or by certain administrative practices or decrees. This is the case in Bosnia and Herzegovina, Bulgaria, Croatia, Estonia, France, Georgia, Hungary, Iceland, Lithuania, Luxembourg, Moldova, Poland and Serbia.

However, in some of the states where legislation is in place, such legislation is not always clear in its scope. For example, some laws appear to confuse the legal recognition of the preferred gender with procedures regulating access to gender reassignment treatment. In other instances laws are not implemented – in Ukraine, NGOs report that the medical board in charge of deciding on applications from transgender persons did not meet once in the period 2007-2008 despite its obligation to meet every three months.[290] In yet other instances, procedures described in laws are not "quick, transparent and accessible" as recommended by the Committee of Ministers. Transgender persons have expressed concern regarding such procedures and the inability to have decisions on their legal gender recognition made subject to judicial review.

Surgery leading to sterilisation as a requirement for legal gender recognition

Some countries require surgery leading to sterilisation before they legally recognise the new gender. It should be stressed that this requirement would also apply in the absence of a medical necessity or the applicant's wish for such surgery. Surgery leading to sterilisation has been identified as a requirement in 29 member states (Belgium, Bosnia and Herzegovina, Bulgaria, Croatia, Cyprus, the Czech Republic, Denmark,[291] Estonia, Finland,[292] France, Georgia, Greece,

---

287. Amendments have been proposed to the Civil Status Document Law allowing for the rectification of the recorded sex in the birth registry, but these proposals have not been adopted. European Union Agency for Fundamental Human Rights, "Homophobia, Transphobia, Discrimination on Grounds of Sexual Orientation and Gender Identity: 2010 Update – A Comparative Legal Analysis", 2010, p. 15.
288. However, (aspects of) the law have been declared unconstitutional in Germany and Austria, therefore these member states will have to adapt their laws or develop new legislation.
289. However, the Irish Government has stated in its government programme that it "will ensure that transgender people will have legal recognition and extend the protections of the equality legislation to them". See "Towards Recovery: Programme for a National Government 2011-2016", p. 54.
290. National contribution (sociological report) on Ukraine, p. 27.
291. In Denmark a "permission for castration" is required. FRA national contribution (legal report) on Denmark, p. 23.
292. Despite the legally prescribed requirement, there is evidence that cross-hormonal treatment for a minimum period of six months is also accepted as proof of infertility in Finland.

Iceland, Italy, Latvia, Malta, Moldova, Montenegro, the Netherlands, Norway, Poland, Romania, San Marino, Serbia, Slovakia, Sweden, Switzerland,[293] Turkey and Ukraine). In two member states, Austria[294] and Germany,[295] the "sterilisation requirement" has been declared unconstitutional by their respective constitutional courts, but no new legislation has been proposed or adopted. In four member states – Hungary (administrative practice), the United Kingdom, Portugal and Spain (by law) – no requirements of sterilisation are enforced. In the Russian Federation there is also no legal basis for sterilisation, though some civil registry offices or courts have reportedly required sterilisation in order to recognise the new gender. In the remaining 11 member states there is either no legislation regulating legal gender recognition or the situation regarding the sterilisation requirement is unclear (see Map 5.1).

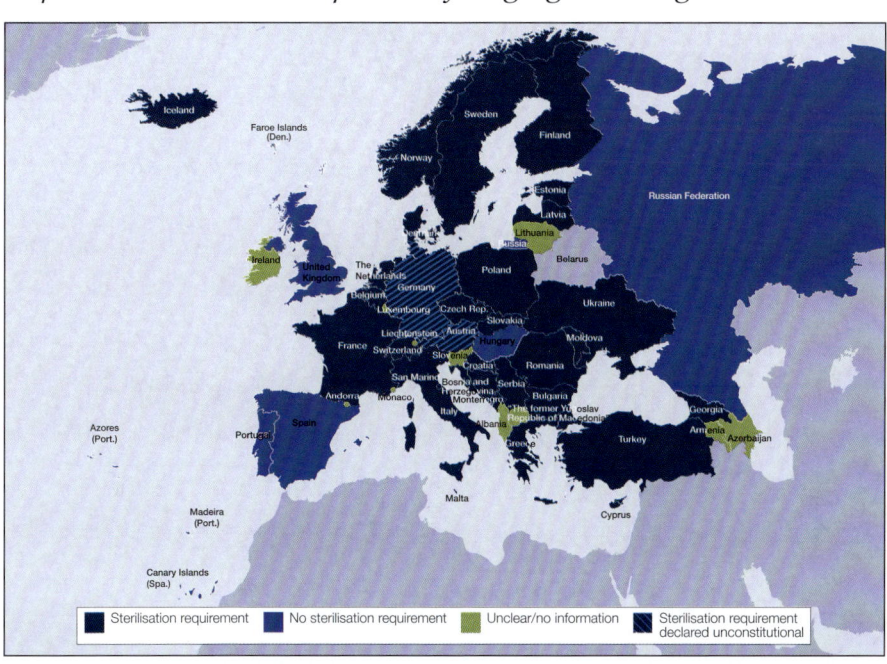

Map 5.1: Sterilisation as a requirement for legal gender recognition

Divorce as a requirement for legal gender recognition

Many member states of the Council of Europe require transgender persons to be unmarried in order to be legally recognised in the preferred gender. In 15 member states (Bulgaria, the Czech Republic, Finland, France, Hungary,

---

293. However, not in all cantons, as the Zurich High Court decided on 1 February 2011 that for the purpose of legal recognition of the preferred gender there is no need to be irreversibly infertile. Cantonal High Court of Zurich (Obergericht des Kantons Zürich), NC090012, 1 February 2011.
294. Constitutional Court of Austria (Verfassungsgerichtshof), V 4/06, 8 June 2006.
295. Federal Constitutional Court of Germany (Bundesverfassungsgericht), 1 BvR 3295/07, 11 January 2011.

Iceland, Italy, Malta, Poland, Serbia, Sweden, Switzerland,[296] Turkey, Ukraine and the United Kingdom) the person who applies for a rectification of the recorded sex has to be unmarried. This entails mandatory divorce if the person is already married. Divorce is not required by six member states (Belgium, Georgia, the Netherlands, Portugal, Romania and Spain). In the Russian Federation there is also no legal requirement for divorce though some transgender persons reported that the existence of a marriage was regarded as an obstacle to be legally recognised in the new gender.

In the remaining 25 member states the information regarding the divorce requirement is either unclear or there is no legislation in force (see Map 5.2).

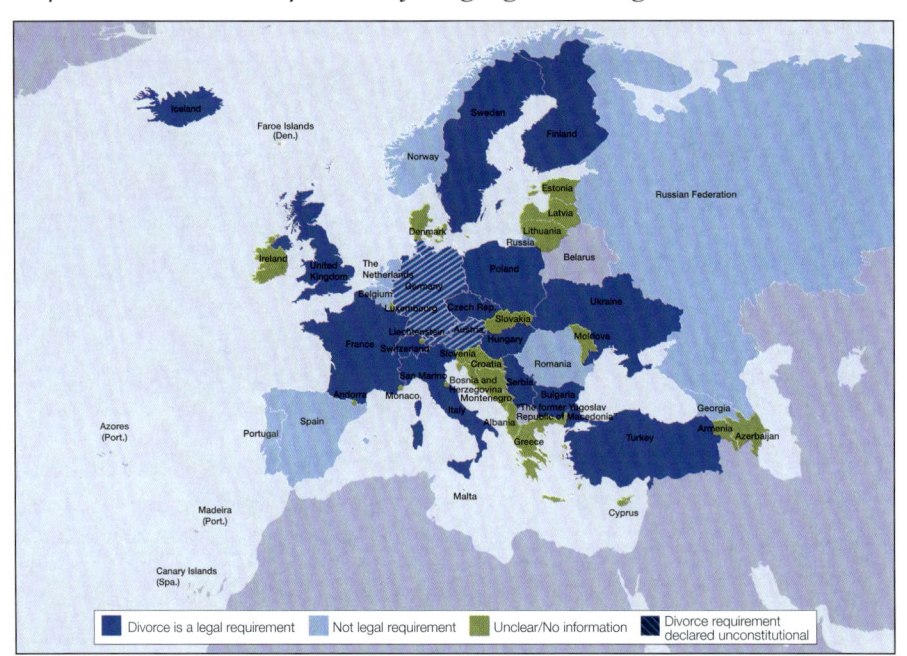

Map 5.2: Divorce as a requirement for legal gender recognition

While the European Court of Human Rights has given a wide margin of appreciation to member states which require the unmarried status for legal gender recognition,[297] it has also acknowledged that such legislation "clearly puts transgender persons in a quandary" since they have effectively to choose between gender recognition or remaining married.[298] Rulings by the highest courts in some member states, however, point in a different direction. The

---

296. Only some cantons in Switzerland require divorce.
297. European Court of Human Rights, *Parry v. United Kingdom*, Application No. 42971/05, Admissibility Decision, 28 November 2006; *R. and F. v. United Kingdom*, Application No. 35748/05, Admissibility Decision, 28 November 2006.
298. A case is pending before the European Court of Human Rights. In the communicated case *H. v. Finland*, Application No. 37359/09, the applicant complained, *inter alia*, that she could not change her identity number unless she divorced her wife.

Austrian Constitutional Court granted a transgender woman the right to change her sex to female while remaining married to her wife. It ruled that "changing a sex entry in a birth certificate cannot be hindered by marriage".[299] The German Constitutional Court in 2008 ruled that change of sex on a birth certificate should not lead to a mandatory divorce, resulting in a decision[300] that prompted a change in the German law and ended compulsory divorce for married couples in which one partner is transgender.

Change of name

Transgender persons may wish to change their first name regardless of their desire to undergo gender reassignment treatment. In order to be eligible for a change of first name, there are similar patterns to some of the procedures described above for legal gender recognition. However, in some countries a name change is easier to obtain since most countries have general provisions for a name change in their law – also for non-transgender persons who want to change their first or last name. A problem arises, however, that in some countries there is a limited choice of names available for the purpose. Reportedly in some member states only gender-neutral names can be chosen while in other member states the opposite is true: no gender-neutral names are allowed.

Generally, member states require some form of medical opinion. Some states allow a change of name on documents only on production of a certificate from the medical profession confirming that gender reassignment surgery has taken place or evidence of the legal gender recognition (for example Croatia, Georgia, Latvia, Moldova, San Marino, Slovakia and Ukraine). At least three other member states require proof of hormonal treatment (Belgium, Croatia and Switzerland). In yet other states applicants need to have a gender dysphoria diagnosis to qualify for the name change (Denmark, Germany, Finland and some cantons in Switzerland). In some states such as Malta a court authorisation is required for a change of name. In the United Kingdom and Ireland a certificate from a notary is sufficient to secure a legal name change. In Ireland, it is remarkable that while it is impossible to receive legal gender recognition, there is a relatively simple procedure for a name change.

Privacy is not always respected during such processes. For example, in Croatia, the Personal Names Act[301] prescribes that after receiving a request for a change of name, the municipal administrative body is obliged to publish an announcement of the submitted request on a public notice board. The State Registries Act then prescribes that a change of personal name and sex are entered as additional entries. This means that if a person changes her name from Marko to Ana, she will have a birth certificate in which 'Marko'

---

299. Constitutional Court of Austria (Verfassungsgerichtshof), V 4/06, 8 June 2006.
300. Federal Constitutional Court of Germany (Bundesverfassungsgericht), 1 BvL 10/05, 27 May 2008.
301. Personal Names Act, OG, No. 69/92.

will be entered in the basic entry, and below, in small letters at the bottom of the document, the following note would be added: "By the decision of the municipal administrative body No. ..., the name was changed to Ana on the date ... ."). As a result, all citizens are able to find out about the applicant's change of gender and name when the data is published on the notice board, and later on that information is also visible in birth certificates.

The difficulty of living with documents that reflect the wrong gender identity or wrong name cannot be exaggerated. Transgender persons who have been unable to change their passport or ID experience problems every time they have to identify themselves, for example when paying with a credit card, taking out a library book, opening a bank account or crossing a border. As a result of having inadequate documents, transgender persons can spend long periods of life effectively barred from meaningful and full participation in society, education or employment, as they may face continual problems "justifying" their identities. Transgender persons may also face practical problems in institutional settings such as hospitals, public toilets, police stations[302] and prisons.

Even after transgender persons have achieved legal gender recognition and the change of name, the problems with privacy may not always disappear – for example when transgender persons are unable to change their name and gender on their diplomas and other educational documents. Some graduate transgender persons have had difficulty changing the sex or name on diplomas that were issued before their gender was legally recognised. The Ministry of Education in the Netherlands has ordered all universities to change graduates' diplomas on legal gender recognition, after the University of Amsterdam lost a case against a former student at the Equal Treatment Commission in 2010.[303] The Committee of Ministers in its Recommendation R(2010)5 has explicitly stipulated that member states should provide effective protection of privacy of transgender persons in relation to, for example, employment applications, and with regard to disclosure of the gender identity history.[304] However, in a survey in Scotland (United Kingdom) "40% of transgender respondents rated the services of their human resources departments as "extremely poor (…) and 15% felt that their employer failed to protect their privacy".[305]

---

302. For example, in France, a transgender woman whose ID papers indicated that she is male complained that she was put in the male ward of a prison. Communication received by the Office of the Commissioner for Human Rights.
303. Dutch Equal Treatment Commission, Decision No. 2010-175, 30 November 2010.
304. Committee of Ministers Recommendation R(2010)5 on measures to combat discrimination on grounds of sexual orientation or gender identity, paragraphs 29 and 30.
305. Scottish Transgender Alliance, "Transgender Experiences in Scotland – Research Summary", Equality Network, Edinburgh, 2008, pp. 14-15, also quoted in European Union Agency for Fundamental Human Rights, "Homophobia and Discrimination on Grounds of Sexual Orientation and Gender Identity in the European Union Member States: Part II – The Social Situation", 2009, p. 117.

5.3. The right to marry and legally contract a partnership

European standards and the national situation

Same-sex couples do not as yet have the right to marry under international human rights law, but their legal rights have evolved through changes in national legislation and recent European jurisprudence. In the case of *Schalk and Kopf v. Austria* in June 2010, the European Court of Human Rights recognised for the first time that same-sex partners enjoy "family life" in the sense of Article 8 of the European Convention on Human Rights. Seven member states (Belgium, Iceland, the Netherlands, Norway, Portugal, Spain and Sweden) have given same-sex partners access to marriage (see Map 5.3). Thirteen others have introduced a form of registered partnership (Andorra, Austria, the Czech Republic, Denmark, Finland, France, Germany, Hungary, Ireland, Luxembourg, Slovenia, Switzerland and the United Kingdom). Croatia has introduced a system of cohabitation rights for same-sex partners. The Parliament of Liechtenstein approved the Bill on Registered Partnership on 16 March 2011.[306]

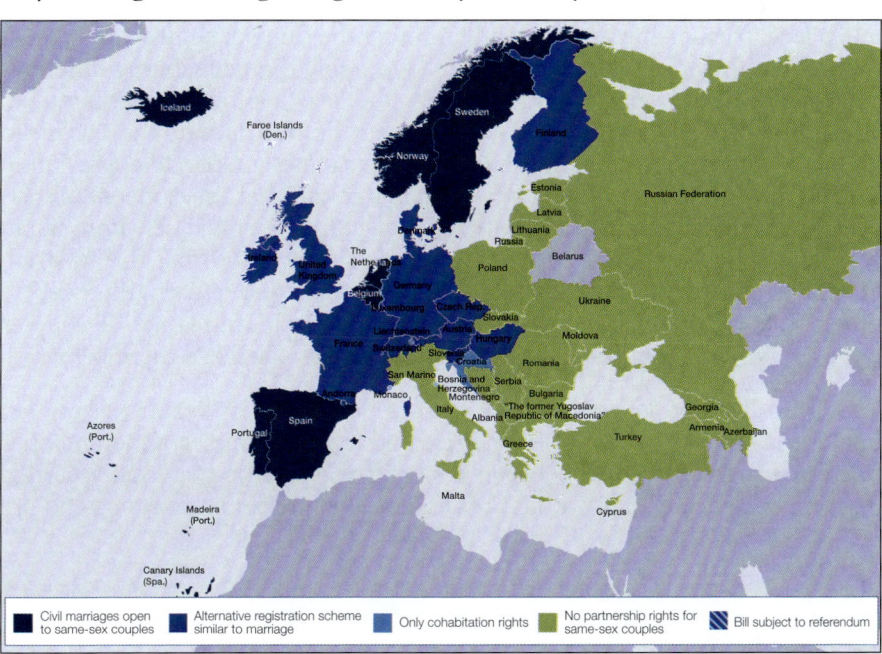

Map 5.3: Legislation regarding same-sex partnerships

The remaining 25 member states (Albania, Armenia, Azerbaijan, Bosnia and Herzegovina, Bulgaria, Cyprus, Estonia, Georgia, Greece, Italy, Latvia, Lithuania, Malta, Moldova, Monaco, Montenegro, Poland, Romania, the Russian Federation, San Marino, Serbia, Slovakia, "the former Yugoslav Republic of

---

306. The bill is subject to a referendum.

Macedonia", Turkey and Ukraine) do not legally recognise same-sex couples through marriage, partnership registration or cohabitation rights. Some of these member states (Bulgaria, Latvia, Moldova, Lithuania, Montenegro, Serbia, Ukraine and Romania) have specified that marriage is the prerogative of different-sex couples.[307]

Some member states would refuse to recognise same-sex partnerships and marriages concluded abroad. Others wish to avoid having their nationals enter a same-sex partnership abroad at all. Before they register a partnership or marriage abroad Polish citizens, for example, usually need to present a certificate from the Polish Civil Status Office confirming that they are unmarried. The Ministry of Internal Affairs and Administration of Poland has instructed[308] that certificates will be issued only to persons wishing to enter a different-sex marriage. Lesbian women, bisexual or gay men wishing to enter a marriage or partnership abroad must obtain special notary certificates at additional cost and effort. A petition of Polish NGOs on this subject was presented on 31 May 2010 to the European Parliament Petitions Committee, which is examining it.

States that do not give same-sex couples the opportunity to marry or to enter into a legal partnership arrangement granting the same or similar rights must ensure that they do not treat them less favourably than cohabiting different-sex couples in the same situation, unless the less favourable treatment can be justified by very weighty reasons.[309] Over the last decade, the European Court of Human Rights has gradually narrowed states' margin of appreciation in this area. In the case of *Karner v. Austria* it found that the Convention had been breached when Austria terminated the tenancy of someone whose same-sex partner had just died. In the ruling, the Court found that the Austrian Government had failed to advance any arguments (particularly the need to protect the "traditional family") that showed that excluding same-sex couples from the provisions of the Rent Act was necessary to achieve its objective.[310]

The Court has not yet ruled with regard to differences in treatment between unmarried same-sex couples and married different-sex couples, although it has ruled that such differences between same-sex registered partners and married different-sex partners fall within the margin of appreciation of states and are

---

307. National contributions (legal reports) on the relevant member states; European Union Agency for Fundamental Human Rights, "Homophobia, Transphobia, Discrimination on Grounds of Sexual Orientation and Gender Identity: 2010 Update – A Comparative Legal Analysis", 2010, pp. 46-47.
308. Instruction of the Deputy Director of the Department for Information Technology Development and State Registers of the Ministry of the Interior and Administration of 3 April 2002, No. DIR-V-6000-21-2731/2002.
309. The Court also held in other cases that, where a difference of treatment is based on sexual orientation, the margin afforded to the state is narrow. See, for example, European Court of Human Rights, *E. B. v. France*, Application No. 43546/02, paragraphs 91 and 93, *S. L. v. Austria*, Application No. 45330/99, judgment of 9 January 2003, paragraph 37, *Smith and Grady v. United Kingdom*, Applications Nos. 33985/96 and 33986/96, judgment of 27 September 1999, paragraphs 89 and 94; *Karner v. Austria*, Application No. 40016/98, judgment of 24 July 2003, paragraphs 37 and 41, and *Kozak v. Poland*, Application No. 13102/02, judgment of 2 March 2010, paragraph 92.
310. European Court of Human Rights, *Karner v. Austria*, Application No. 40016/98, judgment of 24 July 2003, paragraph 92.

therefore permissible.[311] In its Recommendation CM/Rec(2010)5, the Committee of Ministers recalls and reiterates the case law of the Court and recommends as follows: "Where States grant rights and obligations to unmarried couples, these should apply equally to same-sex couples; where States grant rights and obligations to same-sex couples through registered partnerships, these should be the same as for heterosexual couples in a comparable situation; and where neither of these situations apply, States should consider the possibility of providing same-sex couples with legal or other means to address the practical problems related to the social reality in which they live."[312]

Transgender persons' right to marry

Case law from the European Court of Human Rights on the right of transsexual persons to marry has also evolved. Before 2002 it held that the right to marry under Article 12 of the European Convention on Human Rights referred exclusively to marriage between persons of different biological sex.[313] In the case of *Goodwin v. United Kingdom* in 2002, however, it found that the right to marry can no longer depend on a gender determination based only on biological criteria, and should extend to transsexual persons who have undergone gender reassignment surgery and wish to marry a person of the opposite sex after gender reassignment. It found that the United Kingdom had violated the right to marry of a transgender woman when it prevented her from amending her birth certificate and so marrying a male partner.[314] However, transgender persons may still face obstacles in this regard in some member states. For example in Malta in 2007 a transgender woman who had successfully legally changed her sex to "female" on her birth certificate was refused permission to marry her male partner by the Maltese Marriage Registrar on the basis that the applicant was a man and could not be authorised to marry a man. While the applicant's initial request to marry was first upheld by the court, it was later successfully challenged by the Marriage Registrar. In view of this, the applicant filed a constitutional case alleging a violation of her right to marry and the Maltese Constitutional Court decided in her favour on 30 November 2010 citing jurisprudence from the European Court of Human Rights. The Marriage Registrar, however, appealed this decision on 17 December 2010.[315]

---

311. European Court of Human Rights, *Schalk and Kopf v. Austria*, Application No. 30141/04, judgment of 24 June 2010, paragraph 108.
312. Committee of Ministers Recommendation CM/Rec(2010)5 on measures to combat discrimination on grounds of sexual orientation or gender identity, adopted 31 March 2010, paragraphs 23-25.
313. European Court of Human Rights, *Rees v. United Kingdom*, Application No. 9532/81, judgment of 17 October 1986, paragraphs 49-51; *Cossey v. United Kingdom*, Application No. 10843/84, judgment of 27 September 1990, paragraphs 43-48; *Sheffield and Horsham v. United Kingdom*, Applications Nos. 22985/93 and 23390/94, judgment of 30 July 1998 (Grand Chamber), paragraphs 62-70.
314. European Court of Human Rights, *Christine Goodwin v. United Kingdom*, Application No. 28957/95, judgment of 11 July 2002, paragraphs 100-104. See also *I. v. United Kingdom*, Application No. 25680/94, judgment of 11 July 2002.
315. *Cassar Joanne v. Direttur Tar-Registru Pubbliku*, Application No. 43/2008, 30 November 2010, Civil First Hall. The final judgment is pending.

Attitudes and public debate

Access to marriage or other legal recognition to couples of the same sex has been hotly debated across member states in the last few decades. Attitudes towards the legal recognition of same-sex partnerships are most positive in states where LGBT people already receive some level of legal recognition. The Ombudsman in Spain observed a significant increase in the understanding and acceptance of LGBT people in the wake of the political debate surrounding the introduction of marriage for same-sex couples in Spain.[316] A survey carried out in European Union member states in 2006 found the following results (see Map 5.4).[317]

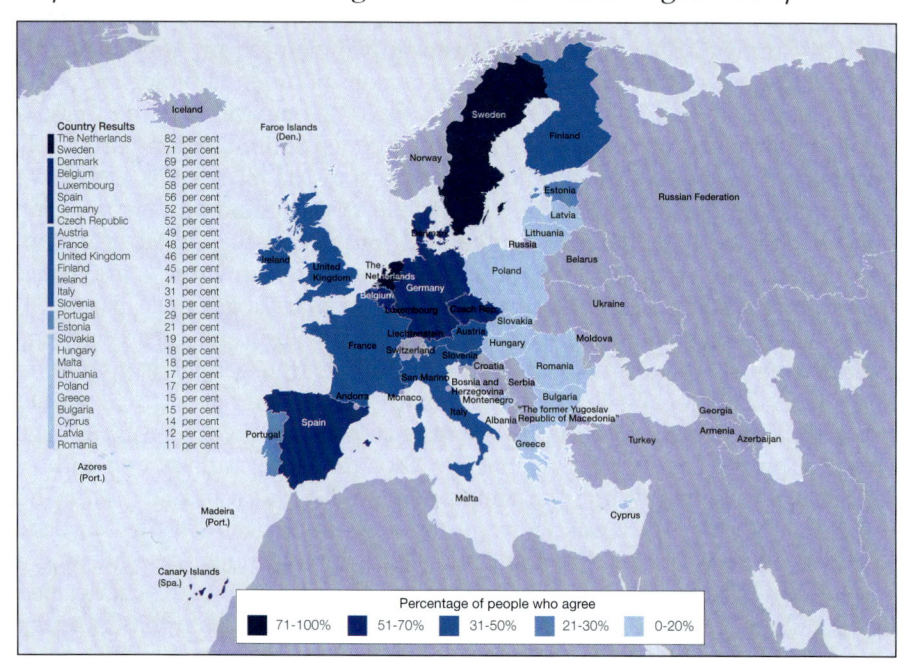

Map 5.4: "Homosexual marriages should be allowed throughout Europe"

Country Results	
The Netherlands	82 per cent
Sweden	71 per cent
Denmark	69 per cent
Belgium	62 per cent
Luxembourg	58 per cent
Spain	56 per cent
Germany	52 per cent
Czech Republic	52 per cent
Austria	49 per cent
France	48 per cent
United Kingdom	46 per cent
Finland	45 per cent
Ireland	41 per cent
Italy	31 per cent
Slovenia	31 per cent
Portugal	29 per cent
Estonia	21 per cent
Slovakia	19 per cent
Hungary	18 per cent
Malta	18 per cent
Lithuania	17 per cent
Poland	17 per cent
Greece	15 per cent
Bulgaria	15 per cent
Cyprus	14 per cent
Latvia	12 per cent
Romania	11 per cent

Percentage of people who agree: 71-100%, 51-70%, 31-50%, 21-30%, 0-20%

In other national surveys results have been mixed. In Montenegro 16% of the population believed that same-sex couples should have the right to marry and 21% that they should be able to register their partnership.[318] In Ukraine 34% of respondents thought that same-sex couples should have rights equal to the rest of the population, and 53% that they never should.[319]

---

316. European Union Agency for Fundamental Rights, "Homophobia and Discrimination on Grounds of Sexual Orientation and Gender Identity in the European Union Member States: Part II – The Social Situation", 2009, p. 31.
317. European Commission, Special Eurobarometer 66, "Public Opinion in the European Union", 2006, pp. 43-44.
318. Human Rights Action, "Homophobia in Montenegro", Ipsos Strategic Marketing, October 2009, p. 5.
319. Our World, "Ukrainian Homosexuals and Society: A Reciprocation – Review of the Situation: Society, Authorities and Politicians, Mass Media, Legal Issues, Gay Community", Kiev, 2007, p. 65.

In Denmark, 82% of the population favoured giving same-sex couples access to marriage.[320]

Impact of non-recognition

LGBT families can face unique challenges when their partnerships are not recognised. Institutions usually assume a different-sex couple or a mother and a father when devising services, benefits and procedures.[321] LGBT families may suffer from stigma in society. Research also identified that lack of legal recognition may lead them to receive inferior tax, employment and insurance benefits, public housing allocations and non-recognition as a second parent from day-care or education services. In cases of serious illness, it is possible too that life partners are unable to get recognition as next of kin and so are excluded from their partner's bedside and hospital decisions about their care. At a day-to-day level, LGBT families may have a poor experience of services – such as schools, day-care centres and health services – that are designed with heterosexual families in mind. This was the experience of 19% of LGBT respondents to a survey in Finland. In response to similar complaints in Sweden, the then Ombudsman for Sexual Orientation Discrimination initiated a revision of all municipal application forms for social security and childcare to remove their heterosexual bias.

Same-sex couples and LGBT families may be restricted in their freedom of movement within Europe as they may not be able to reside with their family members as their family ties are not recognised. Same-sex couples – with or without children – face particular problems if they want to emigrate, work abroad or move for reasons of family reunification. The destination country may not recognise the marriage certificate of a same-sex couple, which is relevant for same-sex couples married in the seven member states who opened civil marriage for same-sex couples. An evaluation of Dutch legislation on registered partnerships and marriage commissioned by the Dutch Ministry of Justice[322] concluded that even though freedom of movement of persons is guaranteed within the European Union, the legal recognition abroad of marriages between same-sex partners is problematic. The situation for same-sex couples under registered partnerships or for those with no access to any form of registered partnership is even more complex. A comparative legal analysis by the European Agency for Fundamental Rights in 2010 notes Europe's "uneven landscape with respect to freedom of movement and family reunification for same-sex couples".[323] It says that the meaning of the term "family member" in the context of free movement, family reunification and asylum

---

320. Westerlund J., "Regnbågsfamiljers ställning i Norden. Politik, rättigheter och villkor", Oslo: Nordiskt institut för kunskap om kön, 2009, p. 131.
321. See, for example, "The Equality Authority for a Diverse Ireland. Implementing Equality for Lesbians, Gays and Bisexuals", 2002.
322. Boele-Woelki K. et al., *Huwelijk of geregistreerd partnerschap?, Evaluatie van de wet openstelling huwelijk en de wet geregistreerd partnerschap*, Kluwer, Deventer, 2007.
323. European Agency for Fundamental Rights, "Homophobia, Transphobia, Discrimination on Grounds of Sexual Orientation and Gender Identity: 2010 Update – A Comparative Legal Analysis", 2010, p. 8.

"often remains vague" although it has been or will be expanded to include same-sex couples to different degrees and in different areas in Austria, France, Ireland, Luxembourg, Portugal and Spain.

5.4. Parenting and children

Many LGBT persons in Council of Europe member states raise children, whether alone or with their partners. They may bring children from previous relationships to their partnership, or they may have adopted children or acquired legal custody over a child. LGBT persons may also have accessed services for medically assisted reproduction. Regardless of the specific form, rights of custody, inheritance and next-of-kin status need to be assured in the best interests of the child. Transgender persons who are parents face particular problems. They may have to divorce in the process of their legal gender recognition and lose custody rights that arose from their married status.

An expert report produced for the Council of Europe focused on the rights and legal status of children brought up in various forms of marital or non-marital partnership or cohabitation. It found that the well-being of children in families of same-sex partners depends not only on the families themselves, but on the legal framework that ensures or limits the stable protection they receive from their carers. It notes:

> *Children do not live in a vacuum, but within a family, and an important part of their protection is that the family unit, no matter what form it takes, enjoys adequate and equal legal recognition and protection. In other words, it is as discriminating to the child to limit legal parenthood, or to deny significant carers legal rights and responsibilities, as it is to accord the child a different status and legal rights according to the circumstances of their birth or upbringing.*[324]

The Committee of Ministers has recommended to member states in its Recommendation CM/Rec(2010)5 that member states make the child's best interests the primary concern when they decide on parental responsibility for or custody over a child, and that any such decisions are taken without discrimination based on sexual orientation or gender identity.[325]

Adoption

The UN Convention on the Rights of the Child sets the legally binding, international standards for adoption. Inter-country adoptions are further regulated by the 1993 Hague Convention. In the European context, the 2008 European Convention on the Adoption of Children (revised) addresses the scope for

---

[324]. Lowe N., "A study into the Rights and Legal Status of Children Being Brought Up in Various Forms of Marital or Non-Marital Partnerships and Cohabitation", Directorate General of Human Rights and Legal Affairs, Council of Europe Secretariat, 2010, p. 3.

[325]. Committee of Ministers Recommendation CM/Rec(2010)5 on measures to combat discrimination on grounds of sexual orientation or gender identity, adopted on 31 March 2010, paragraph 26.

considering same-sex couples as adoptive parents.[326] It finds that states may permit a child to be adopted by couples of the same sex who are married to each other, or who have entered into a registered partnership. States can also extend the scope of this convention to different-sex couples and to same-sex couples who are living together in a stable relationship.[327] The European Court of Human Rights has held that adoption means "providing a child with a family, not a family with a child" and where the interests of the child compete with those who want to adopt, the best interests of the child shall be decisive.[328] The Court has found that distinctions drawn on the basis of sexual orientation are unacceptable under the convention in (single-parent) adoption cases[329] as it had also already done in a case regarding child custody.[330] The Committee of Ministers has recommended states that if they permit single individuals to adopt, they should be sure to apply the law without discrimination on grounds of sexual orientation or gender identity.[331]

LGBT persons can adopt a child by one of three procedures. A single lesbian woman or gay man may apply to become an adoptive parent (single-parent adoption). Alternatively, a same-sex couple can adopt their partner's biological or adopted children without terminating the first parent's legal rights. These are called "second-parent adoptions" and give the child two legal guardians. Second-parent adoptions also protect the parents by giving both of them legally recognised parental status. The lack of second-parent adoption deprives the child and the non-biological parent of rights if the biological parent dies or in the case of divorce, separation, or other circumstances that would bar the parent from carrying out parental responsibilities. The child also has no right to inherit from the non-biological parent. Moreover, at an everyday level, the lack of second-parent adoption rules out parental leave, which can be harmful financially for LGBT families. The third procedure is joint adoption of a child by a same-sex couple.

Ten member states allow second-parent adoption to same-sex couples (Belgium, Denmark, Finland, Germany, Iceland, the Netherlands, Norway, Spain, Sweden and the United Kingdom). Apart from Finland and Germany these member states also give access to joint adoptions for same-sex couples. In Austria and France there is no access to second-parent adoption but same-sex couples in registered partnerships are allowed some parental authority or responsibilities. No access to joint adoption or second-parent adoption is a reality in 35 member

---

326. European Convention on the Adoption of Children (revised), Strasbourg, 27 November 2008 (CETS No. 202), opened for signature in November 2008.
327. Ibid., Article 7.
328. European Court of Human Rights, *Pini and others v. Romania*, Applications Nos. 78028/01 and 78030/01, judgment of 22 June 2004, paragraphs 155-56.
329. See, for example, European Court of Human Rights, *E. B. v. France*, Application No. 43546/02, paragraphs 91 and 93, judgment of 22 January 2000.
330. European Court of Human Rights, *Salgueiro Da Silva Mouta v. Portugal*, Application No. 33290/96, judgment of 21 December 1999, paragraph 34.
331. Committee of Ministers Recommendation CM/Rec(2010)5 on measures to Combat Discrimination on Grounds of Sexual Orientation or Gender Identity, adopted on 31 March 2010, paragraph 27.

states: Albania, Andorra, Armenia, Azerbaijan, Bosnia and Herzegovina, Bulgaria, Croatia, Cyprus, the Czech Republic, Estonia, Georgia, Greece, Hungary, Ireland, Italy, Latvia, Liechtenstein, Lithuania, Luxembourg, Malta, Moldova, Monaco, Montenegro, Poland, Portugal, Romania, the Russian Federation, San Marino, Serbia, Slovakia, Slovenia, Switzerland, "the former Yugoslav Republic of Macedonia", Turkey and Ukraine (see Map 5.5).

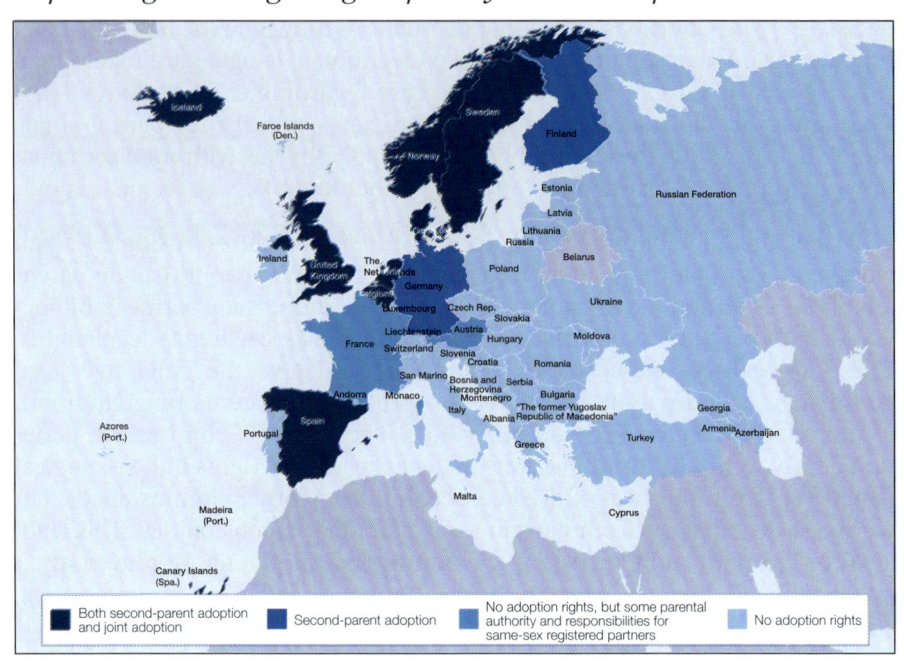

Map 5.5: Legislation regarding adoption by same-sex couples

Assisted reproduction

Some same-sex couples become parents by using available techniques of assisted reproduction, which are also accessible for different-sex couples. Access to assisted reproduction is not explicitly mentioned in any legally binding human rights instrument. In its case law, the European Court of Human Rights has not identified a positive obligation for states to ensure a right to assisted reproduction. In the case of *Marckx v. Belgium* the Court held that "by guaranteeing the right to respect for family life, Article 8 presupposes the existence of a family".[332] The Court added that Article 8 of the Convention did not cover the aspiration to become a parent.[333]

---

332. European Court of Human Rights, *Marckx v. Belgium*, Application No. 6833/74, judgment of 13 June 1979, paragraph 31.
333. European Commission of Human Rights, *Di Lazzaro v. Italy*, Application No. 31924/96, decision of 10 July 1997; *X & Y v. UK*, Application No. 7229/75, decision of 15 December 1977. In the second case the Court stated that "Article 12 does not guarantee a right to adopt or otherwise integrate into a family a child which is not the natural child of the couple concerned".

States, however, need very weighty reasons for denying assisted reproduction facilities on the ground of the sexual orientation of a single lesbian woman, where such facilities are provided to single heterosexual women. This follows from the Court's argumentation in *E. B. v. France*, in which it concluded that the refusal of adoption to a single lesbian woman – which would not have applied had she been heterosexual – led to a distinction drawn from her sexual orientation that violated the principle of non-discrimination.[334] The Committee of Ministers has recommended that member states which permit single women assisted reproductive treatment ensure access to such treatment "without any discrimination on the grounds of sexual orientation".[335] Some Council of Europe member states, including Belgium, Denmark, Finland, Iceland, the Netherlands, Norway, Spain, Sweden and the United Kingdom[336] give lesbian couples access to assisted reproduction. Other states make these services available only to married different-sex couples. Denmark banned assisted insemination for women in same-sex couples and for single women in 1997, but reinstated the right in 2007. In Italy, donor insemination was made illegal in 2004 for single women and women living in long-term de facto relationships, among them lesbians.[337]

Attitudes towards parenting of LGBT persons

Research and attitudinal surveys on parenting and adoption have generally centred on whether same-sex couples can make "suitable" parents and whether an LGBT family background has a negative impact on children. Opinion has polarised on both scores. In 2006 the Eurobarometer found an extreme range of views across countries about adoption by same-sex couples (see Map 5.6). It ranged from 7% acceptance in Poland and Malta to over 50% in Sweden and 69% in the Netherlands.[338] Among those most receptive to adoption by same-sex couples were people under 55 years of age, those with the longest formal education, and those who placed themselves on the left of the political spectrum.[339]

---

334. European Court of Human Rights, *E.B. v. France*, Application No. 43546/02, paragraphs 91 and 93, judgment of 22 January 2008.
335. Committee of Ministers Recommendation CM/Rec(2010)5 on measures to Combat Discrimination on Grounds of Sexual Orientation or Gender Identity, adopted on 31 March 2010, paragraph 28.
336. Overview based on national contributions (legal reports). Also ILGA-Europe, Rainbow Europe Map and Country Index, 2010.
337. FRA national contribution (sociological report) on Italy, p. 8.
338. European Union Agency for Fundamental Rights, "Homophobia and Discrimination on Grounds of Sexual Orientation and Gender Identity in the EU Member States: Part II – The Social Situation", 2009, pp. 31-32.
339. European Commission, Special Eurobarometer 66, "Public Opinion in the European Union", 2006, pp. 45-46.

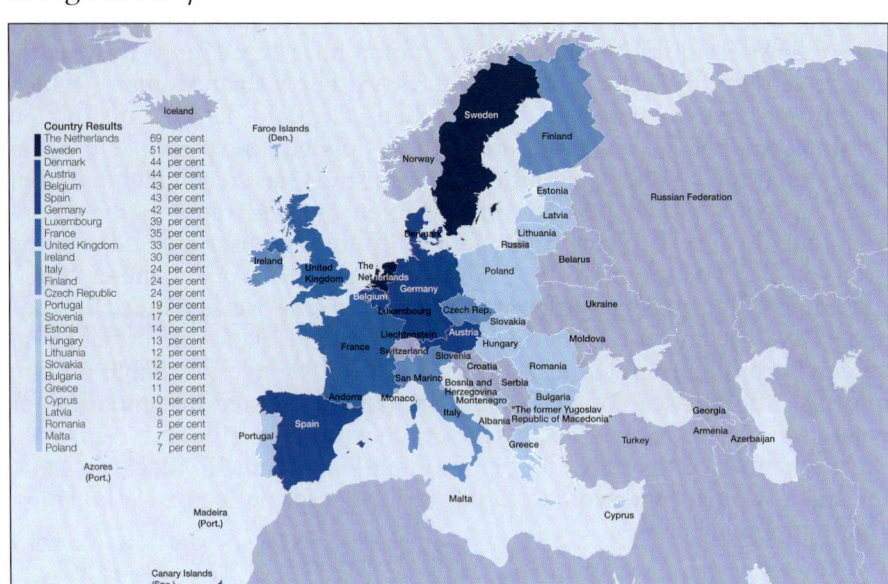

Map 5.6: "Adoption of children should be authorised for homosexual couples throughout Europe"

Country Results	
The Netherlands	69 per cent
Sweden	51 per cent
Denmark	44 per cent
Austria	44 per cent
Belgium	43 per cent
Spain	43 per cent
Germany	42 per cent
Luxembourg	39 per cent
France	35 per cent
United Kingdom	33 per cent
Ireland	30 per cent
Italy	24 per cent
Finland	24 per cent
Czech Republic	24 per cent
Portugal	19 per cent
Slovenia	17 per cent
Estonia	14 per cent
Hungary	13 per cent
Lithuania	12 per cent
Slovakia	12 per cent
Bulgaria	12 per cent
Greece	11 per cent
Cyprus	10 per cent
Latvia	8 per cent
Romania	8 per cent
Malta	7 per cent
Poland	7 per cent

Percentage of people who agree: 51-100%, 41-50%, 31-40%, 21-30%, 0-20%

Surveys from other member states have been patchy. In Montenegro, 12% of the population favoured giving same-sex couples access to adoption and 24% of students.[340] According to an Icelandic survey in 2000, 53% of the population were in favour of giving lesbians and gay men access to adoption.[341]

One argument put forward by opponents of parenting by LGBT persons is that it is natural and in a child's best interest to have a father and a mother. This line of thinking assumes that LGBT parenting harms children and cannot ensure their well-being. According to a 2001 Swedish Government report "combined research shows that children with LGBT parents have developed psychologically and socially in a similar way to the children with which they were compared. No differences emerged either as regards the children's sexual development. Nor did any difference emerge from the research between the ability of homosexual and heterosexual parents to offer children good nurturing and care".[342] A German research digest in 2009 found that:

– the sexual orientation of the parent does not affect the behaviour and development of the child;

---

340. Human Rights Action, "Homophobia in Montenegro", October 2010. Ipsos Strategic Marketing, 2009, p. 5.
341. Westerlund, J., "Regnbågsfamiljers ställning I Norden. Politik, rättigheter och villkor", Oslo: Nordiskt institut för kunskap om kön, 2009, p. 269.
342. The Commission on the Situation of Children in Families, "Children in Families – Summary", official Swedish Government reports, Stockholm, 2001, pp. 6-7.

- children of same-sex parents sometimes suffer from discrimination but have the psychological strength to withstand it;
- children of same-sex parents are more tolerant of homosexuality but no more likely than the national average to become gay themselves.[343]

"Coming out" in the family

Aspects of parenting also come into play from the perspective of the "coming out" of a family member as lesbian, gay, bisexual or transgender. This applies especially to young people who grow up and live with their families and who may at some point discover their sexual orientation or gender identity. In a online survey 47% of Lithuanian LGB persons replied that their families do not know about their sexual orientation.[344] In Georgia, NGO research demonstrates that 87% of LGB persons conceal their sexual orientation to their families.[345] A survey in Serbia shows that 70% of the population would not want one of their relatives to be gay or lesbian.[346] In Croatia, 14% of men surveyed and 3% of women said they would disown a gay son.[347]

The family may be experienced by LGBT persons as an institution of immediate social control. This imposes expectations on the gender roles of boys and girls alike, which can be problematic for LGBT children who do not meet them. NGO representatives in Armenia, Azerbaijan, Georgia and Turkey stressed the double discrimination facing lesbians and bisexual women in those states. As women, they are expected to marry and have children, and until they do they must come home directly from the workplace and not go out alone. Family honour is an influential concept.

In some member states, lack of acceptance by family members can lead to spells of homelessness for young LGBT persons. A study from the United Kingdom showed that 29% of lesbian respondents and 25% of gay ones had to leave their parents' home after "coming out".[348] Young people forced to leave home after "coming out" in Albania and Moldova, where children often live at home until they marry, had difficulty finding accommodation. Similarly, transgender persons report problems after "coming out" to their families. In the United Kingdom a study found that 45% of respondents experienced a breakdown of their relationship with their family as a result.[349]

---

343. Eggen B., "Gleichgeschlechtliche Lebensgemeinschaften mit und ohne Kinder. Eine Expertise auf der Basis des Mikrozensus 2006", Staatsinstitut fur Familienforschung an der Universitat Bamberg, 2009.
344. FRA national contribution (sociological report) on Lithuania, p.7.
345. Inclusive Foundation, Discrimination survey conducted among 120 LGBT in Georgia – February 2006.
346. Gay Straight Alliance, "Prejudices Exposed – Homophobia in Serbia". Public Opinion Research report on LGBT population, 2008. February-March 2008, p. 2.
347. Lesbian Group Kontra, "Violence against Lesbians, Gays and Bisexuals in Croatia: Research Report", Zagreb, 2006, p. 7.
348. Averill S., "How Can Young People be Empowered to Achieve Justice when they Experience Homophobic Crime?", Middlesex University, 2004, pp. 20-21.
349. Whittle S., Turner L. and Al-Alami M., "Engendered Penalties: Transgender and Transsexual People's Experience of Inequality and Discrimination", Wetherby: The Equalities Review, 2007, p. 68.

6. Access to health care, education and employment

6.1. Introduction

Access to health care, education and employment is crucial to each person's life and well-being. In early life, access to school and consequently education as a means to access paid work can make goods and services available that are indispensable to adult life. In retirement, access to work-related pension and other benefits contribute to a person's autonomy. Underpinning both education and employment is access to health care and the right to the highest attainable standard of health. Access to health care, education and employment are thus interlinked. In fact, a standard of living that is adequate for a person's health is impossible without basic social services and housing as well as food, clothing and medical care, as highlighted by Article 25 of the Universal Declaration of Human Rights.

This chapter considers how LGBT persons in the Council of Europe member states enjoy these three rights in light of the fact that international standards prohibit discriminatory access to health care, education and employment on grounds of sexual orientation or gender identity.[350] In practice, however, this chapter will demonstrate that several impediments prevent LGBT persons from enjoying these rights in a full and effective way.

6.2.　Health

The right to enjoy the highest attainable standard of health involves both entitlements and freedoms. Among entitlements is a system of health protection that makes facilities available to all people without discrimination on any grounds. Freedoms include the right to control one's own body including one's sexual and reproductive freedom, and to be free from non-consensual medical treatment, experimentation and torture. The UN Committee on Economic, Social and Cultural Rights underlines both dimensions in a general comment adopted in 2002, which recognises sexual orientation[351] as a prohibited ground for discrimination in accessing the highest attainable standard of health. In 2009 it explicitly recognised gender identity among the prohibited grounds as well.[352]

---

350. Three General Comments from the UN Committee on Economic, Social and Cultural Rights confirm this: General Comment No. 14, The Right to the Highest Attainable Standard of Health, paragraphs. 8, 12(b), 18, and General Comment No. 20, Non-Discrimination in Economic, Cultural and Social Rights, paragraph 32, and General Comment No. 13, The Right to Education, paragraphs 1, 6d and 37.
351. UN Committee on Economic, Social and Cultural Rights, General Comment No. 14, The Right to the Highest Attainable Standard of Health, paragraph 8.
352. UN Committee on Economic, Social and Cultural Rights, General Comment No. 20, Non-Discrimination in Economic, Cultural and Social Rights, paragraph 32.

Different UN special rapporteurs have cited these standards. In 2009 the UN Special Rapporteur on the Right of Everyone to Enjoy the Highest Attainable Standard of Physical and Mental Health emphasised the stigma on vulnerable communities such as LGBT people that "prevents legislative and policymaking institutions from addressing their health-related matters adequately".[353] He went on to note that attempts to "cure" those who engage in same-sex conduct are not only "inappropriate", but could potentially cause significant psychological distress and increase "stigmatisation". In 2001 the UN Special Rapporteur on Torture and Other Cruel, Inhuman or Degrading Treatment or Punishment referred to reports that "members of sexual minorities have received inadequate medical treatment in public hospitals – even after having been victims of assault – on grounds of their gender identity".[354]

Since 2007 three recommendations of the Committee of Ministers included references to the right of LGBT persons to health protection.[355] Among other things, they recommended the member states to "take appropriate legislative and other measures to ensure that the highest attainable standard of health can be effectively enjoyed without discrimination on grounds of sexual orientation or gender identity" and also to "take into account the specific needs of lesbian, gay, bisexual and transgender persons in the development of national health plans, including suicide prevention measures, health surveys, medical curricula, training courses and materials and when monitoring and evaluating the quality of health care services".[356]

A question of definition

As a whole, the threat of non-consensual medical intervention has decreased for lesbian, gay and bisexual persons since the WHO removed homosexuality from its *International Classification of Diseases* in 1990.[357] Nevertheless, this report found that these outdated classifications still influence medical practice as well as the contents of educational materials in schools, evidenced by examples identified in some of the Council of Europe member states, including Montenegro, the Russian Federation, Serbia, Croatia and Turkey. Not only was such information found in secondary school textbooks, but also in academic

---

353. Human Rights Council, "Report of the Special Rapporteur on the Right of Everyone to the Enjoyment of the Highest Attainable Standard of Physical and Mental Health, Anand Grover", A/HRC/14/20, 27 April 2010, paragraphs 22-23. In 2004 the (then) UN Special Rapporteur, Paul Hunt, also raised concerns regarding LGBT persons' access to health; see E/CN.4/2004/49, paragraph 24 and Hunt P. and de Mesquita J., "The Rights to Sexual and Reproductive Health", University of Essex, 2006, p. 7.
354. "Report of the UN Special Rapporteur on the Question of Torture and Other Cruel, Inhuman or Degrading Treatment or Punishment", UN Doc. A/56/156, 3 July 2001, paragraph 22.
355. Committee of Ministers Recommendation CM/Rec(2007)17 on gender equality standards and mechanisms, adopted on 21 November 2007; Committee of Ministers Recommendation CM/Rec(2010)5 on measures to combat discrimination on grounds of sexual orientation or gender identity, adopted on 31 March 2010; Committee of Ministers Recommendation Rec(2006)18 on health services in a multicultural society, adopted on 8 November 2006.
356. Committee of Ministers Recommendation CM/Rec(2010)5 on measures to combat discrimination on grounds of sexual orientation or gender identity, adopted on 31 March 2010, section VII. Health, paragraph 33.
357. The World Health Organization, International Classification of Diseases, 1990.

literature for medical students. NGOs report that some psychotherapists are still addressing the homosexuality of their clients as a medical or psychiatric problem. In Turkey the military still considers homosexuality as pathology rendering men "unfit to serve" in the armed forces.[358] Gay or bisexual men who apply for exemption from military service undergo "degrading medical and psychological tests"[359] or have to prove their homosexuality, which may have an impact on their future job prospects if applying to work for the authorities.

Two other classification schemes have direct influence on the way Council of Europe member states approach transgender persons when they want to access gender reassignment treatment. The WHO considers transsexualism as a "mental and behavioural disorder"[360] and the American Psychiatric Association[361] includes the term "gender identity disorder" among mental health disorders. Both schemes categorise transgender persons as mentally disordered. Such definitions could influence, for example, the way the military perceives transgender persons as evidenced by a regulation issued by the Bulgarian Ministry of Defence in which transsexuality is perceived as a sexual disorder, making transgender people unfit for military service.[362]

There is gradually growing support for the view that transgender people should be able to access relevant medical treatment and have their preferred gender legally recognised without a diagnosis of being mentally disordered. The Gender Recognition Act in the United Kingdom supports this view, as do the World Professional Association for Transgender Health and many activists for transgender rights worldwide.[363] The WHO's revision of its medical classification, which is planned for publication in 2013, is an important opportunity for reviewing the place of transsexualism within the classification.

Two Council of Europe member states have announced a revision of their national classification systems. In 2009 the National Board of Health and Welfare in Sweden made changes to its national classification system and in 2010 France announced it would delete transsexuality from the list of "long-term psychiatric conditions".[364] It is, however, too early to assess the impact of the decree in France, where clarifications on the practical implications of the announcement are still needed.

---

358. Armed Forces Health Regulation, Paragraph 17, also quoted in national contribution (sociological report) on Turkey, p. 15.
359. Commission of the European Communities, "Turkey 2008 Progress Report", 2009, p. 26.
360. World Health Organization, *International Statistical Classification of Diseases and Related Health Problems*, Tenth Revision, Version for 2007.
361. American Psychiatric Association, *Diagnostic and Statistical Manual of Mental Disorders*, 4th edn, Text Revision: DSM-IV-TR, Washington, DC, 2000.
362. FRA national contribution (legal report) on Bulgaria, p. 32.
363. The Gender Recognition Act 2004; World Professional Association for Transgender Health, "WPATH De-Psychopatholisation Statement", 26 May 2010; see also "Human Rights and Gender Identity", issue paper published by the Office of the Commissioner for Human Rights, 2009.
364. Décret No. 2010-125 du 8 février 2010 portant modification de l'annexe figurant à l'article D. 322-1 du code de la sécurité sociale relative aux critères médicaux utilisés pour la définition de l'affection de longue durée "affections psychiatriques de longue durée".

The state of health of LGBT persons

According to the few studies on the health situation of LGBT persons conducted in Council of Europe member states, LGBT persons have a higher incidence of poor health than heterosexual persons. A study in Belgium, for instance, found that LGB persons are twice as likely to have a chronic disease as the average citizen, which confirms findings by other studies.[365] A Norwegian report from 2007 shows that young lesbians and gay men often experience loneliness and depression.[366] Another report from Norway of 2006 shows that the relatively high level of bullying, harassment and violence to which LGB youth are exposed is linked with high levels of health risk behaviours: "LGB teenagers who have been exposed to severe physical maltreatment reported higher levels of sexual-risk behaviours, substance abuse, suicide ideation, and loitering about in the city."[367]

Suicide by LGBT persons, especially when they are young, has been identified as an urgent issue. The Parliamentary Assembly of the Council of Europe adopted a resolution in 2008 in which it expressed its concerns that suicide rates among young LGBT persons are significantly higher than among their peers. It notes that this heightened risk is due to the stigmatisation, marginalisation and discrimination which they experience in society.[368]

Studies in member states found an alarmingly high percentage of LGBT persons who had attempted or considered committing suicide. For example, in a Danish study, it was found that the percentage of LGBT persons who had considered (16%) or attempted (11%) suicide is about twice as high as the average population.[369] Of these attempts 61% were carried out by people under 20 years of age and 6% by children under 12.[370] A 2007 Norwegian report found young LGBT persons over-represented among youth with high-risk behaviours and suicide ideation.[371] Similarly, in France an NGO survey found that 34% of young transgender persons aged 16-26 had attempted

---

365. van Heeringen C. and Vincke J. "Suicidal acts and ideation in homosexual and bisexual young people: a study of prevalence and risk factors", *Social Psychiatry and Psychiatric Epidemiology No. 35* (2000), pp. 494-99.
366. Hegna K., "Homo? Betydningen av seksuell erfaring, tiltrekning og identitet for selvmordsforsøk og rusmiddelbruk blant ungdom. En sosiologisk studie", Norsk institutt for forskning om oppvekst, velferd og aldring (NOVA), Rapport 1/07, 2007, Oslo, p. 87.
367. Moseng B. U., "Vold mot lesbiske og homofile tenåringer. En representativ undersøkelse av omfang, risiko og beskyttelse – Ung i Oslo 2006", Norsk institutt for forskning om oppvekst, velferd og aldring (NOVA), Rapport 19/07, Oslo, 2006, p. 53.
368. Parliamentary Assembly of the Council of Europe, Resolution 1608 on Child and teenage suicide in Europe: a serious public health issue, 2008, paragraph 10.
369. Gransell L. and Hansen H., "Lige og ulige? Homoseksuelle, biseksuelle og transkønnedes levevilkår", Copenhagen: CASA and Landsforeningen for bøsser og lesbiske, 2009, p. 121.
370. Moseng B. U., "Vold mot lesbiske og homofile tenåringer. En representativ undersøkelse av omfang, risiko og beskyttelse – Ung i Oslo 2006", Norsk institutt for forskning om oppvekst, velferd og aldring (NOVA), Rapport 19/07, Oslo, 2006, p. 53.
371. Hegna K., "Homo? Betydningen av seksuell erfaring, tiltrekning og identitet for selvmordsforsøk og rusmiddelbruk blant ungdom. En sosiologisk studie", Norsk institutt for forskning om oppvekst, velferd og aldring (NOVA), Rapport 1/07, 2007, Oslo, p. 56.

to commit suicide.[372] A United Kingdom study reported that almost 30% of transgender persons had attempted to end their lives.[373]

Some studies suggest that the share of lesbian and bisexual women participating in screening for breast, cervical and uterine cancer is low possibly because they themselves and medical professionals assume they are low-risk groups. Their vulnerability to HIV/AIDS and other sexually transmitted infections (STIs) is largely unknown and often disregarded in awareness-raising campaigns.[374] Some good practice, however, can be reported from member states such as Ireland, which includes in its health strategy a focus on lesbian and bisexual women in all its campaigns on cancer and STIs. Staff are required to have specialist knowledge of lesbian and bisexual women's health problems and a non-judgmental attitude to their sexual orientation.

Obstacles accessing health care: prejudices, stigmatisation and risk of disclosure

A first obstacle in accessing health care is identified in NGO reports[375] which find a significant level of mistrust between LGBT patients and their health care providers which may lead to LGBT persons not seeking medical care if they need it or withholding information about their sexual orientation or gender identity. For example, in Germany a study showed that lesbian women do not reveal their sexual orientation to health services due to fear of discrimination.[376] A large survey among lesbian and bisexual women in the United Kingdom in 2008 showed that nearly half said they conceal their sexual orientation from health professionals.[377]

Mistrust between LGBT persons and their medical practitioners may be fed by fears that the privacy and confidentiality of one's health status, sexual orientation or gender identity and medical records is not respected. For example in Albania in 2006, after the arrest of some LGBT persons on suspicion of prostitution,[378] the media reported that two of the arrested persons were HIV-positive and printed their police photos. In Ukraine the Police Act permits police offers to "reveal and inform the medical establishments in an established order about persons who constitute a group at risk of HIV/AIDS, and to bring these people, as well as persons infected by HIV/AIDS, by sexually transmitted diseases ... at the request

---

372. Homosexualités & Socialisme, Mouvement d'Affirmation des jeunes Gais, Lesbiennes, Bi et Trans, Enquête sur le vécu des jeunes populations trans en France, 2009, p. 1.
373. Whittle S., Turner L., Combs R. and Rhodes S., "Transgender EuroStudy: Legal Survey and Focus on the Transgender Experience of Health Care", Brussels, 2008, p. 49.
374. ILGA, "Lesbian and Bisexual Women's Health: Common Concerns, Local Issues", 2006, p. 18.
375. Quinn S., "Accessing Health: the Context and the Challenges for LGBT People in Central and Eastern Europe", ILGA-Europe, 2006, p. 57.
376. Dennert G., "Die gesundheitliche Situation lesbischer Frauen in Deutschland: Ergebnisse einer Befragung (Dissertation)", Nürnberg: Med. Diss. FAU Erlangen-Nürnberg, 2004.
377. Hunt R. and Fish J., "Prescription for Change. Lesbian and Bisexual Women's Health Check", Stonewall, 2008, p. 3.
378. National contribution (sociological report) on Albania, p. 8.

of a medical establishment and authorisation of a prosecutor, for a compulsory examination and treatment".[379]

When they seek health care, LGBT persons sometimes perceive that they experience worse treatment in the health service than their peers. For example, reports and statements from NGOs in Albania[380] and Azerbaijan,[381] challenged by the health ministries of both member states,[382] refer to hospitals which allegedly have refused to treat transgender women in accident and emergency departments. In Turkey, the Istanbul Provincial Human Rights Board has reported on similar problems as well as on the lack of privacy for medical examinations of transgender women.[383]

A second obstacle is the prejudiced attitude of medical staff towards LGBT persons, which may be caused by the fact that their knowledge is based on outdated approaches to homosexuality and transgenderism. Doctors may assume that their patients are heterosexual, and if proved otherwise, the medical staff may feel uncomfortable or unduly focus on sexuality, instead of the actual health issues reported by the patients.[384] Several examples of good practice to combat this obstacle can be identified within the Council of Europe member states, for example in the United Kingdom where a guide for health and social care staff who work with transgender persons has been produced.[385] In Sweden educational trainings on LGBT issues have been run by an LGBT NGO and attended by health care students and professionals. In the Russian Federation the Society of Psychoanalytic Therapy has adopted a Code of Ethics that prohibits discrimination on different grounds, including sexual orientation.

A third problem reported is that same-sex partners are not recognised as next of kin in countries that do not grant some form of legal recognition to same-sex partners. In practice it means that patients in life-threatening conditions, or suffering from chronic illness, may find their life partners excluded from decision-making processes about their treatment. Sometimes the partners are not allowed at their bedside. In Estonia, the female partner of a woman who gave birth was not allowed to be present at the birth of the couple's child.[386] A visitor to a gay man living with HIV in a hospital in St Petersburg was report-

---

379. Article 10, paragraph 21 of the Police Act No. 565-12, 20 December 1990.
380. National contribution (sociological report) on Albania, p. 11.
381. "The Violations of the Rights of Lesbian, Gay, Bisexual, Transgender Persons in Azerbaijan", an NGO shadow report presented to the UN Human Rights Committee, July 2009.
382. National contribution (sociological report) on Albania, p. 11 and national contribution (sociological report) on Azerbaijan, p. 15.
383. Report of TC Istanbul Valiliği, Sayı B054VLK4340300/521/37648; national contribution (sociological report) on Turkey, pp. 16-17.
384. Gibbons M., Manandhar M., Gleeson C. and Mullan, J., "Recognising LGB Sexual Identities in Health Services: The Experiences of Lesbian, Gay and Bisexual People with Health Services in North West Ireland". Equality Authority of Ireland, Dublin, 2008, pp. 46-47.
385. *An Introduction to working with transgender people: information for health and social care staff*, Department of Health, United Kingdom, 2007.
386. FRA national contribution (sociological report) on Estonia, p. 8.

edly told by the ward nurse that "this is no place for the meeting of faggots".[387] Other examples from the United Kingdom show that access to a partner's hospital ward can vary according to the discretion of ward staff.[388]

Finally, according to NGOs, gay and bisexual men face situations where they are assumed to be HIV-positive when accessing health services. HIV/AIDS had, and still has, a profound influence on the LGBT community. After being discovered in the 1980s, HIV/AIDS sparked a significant debate and media interest, often using a sensationalist approach referring to HIV/AIDS as the "gay cancer". Despite the fact that the introduction of new medication in the mid 1990s has brought some improvements in living conditions, stigmatisation of persons living with HIV/AIDS is still widespread. In some member states gay and bisexual men have been automatically barred from donating blood. Whereas blood donor centres in some member states have changed their policies and focus on risk behaviours rather than the sexual orientation of the donor, other member states continue to bar gay and bisexual men categorically. The European Court of Human Rights set an important standard when it ruled that an HIV-positive person cannot be refused a residence permit on the basis of his health status.[389]

Specific obstacles for transgender persons when accessing health services

Transgender persons who wish to undergo gender reassignment treatment can face a range of obstacles when trying to access health services. The European Court of Human Rights has established that states have a positive duty to provide for the possibility to undergo gender reassignment as "medically necessary" treatment, which should be covered by insurance schemes. Failure to provide this places a disproportionate burden on a person "in one of the most intimate areas of private life", according to a groundbreaking ruling in 2003.[390] The Court restated this in another case in 2007.[391]

Twenty-eight member states offer full or partial gender reassignment treatment to transgender persons (Austria, Belgium, the Czech Republic, Germany, Denmark, Estonia, Finland, France, Hungary, Greece, Georgia, Iceland, Ireland, Italy, Latvia, Malta, the Netherlands, Norway, Poland, Portugal, the Russian Federation, Serbia, Spain, Sweden, Switzerland, Turkey, the United Kingdom and Ukraine). The differences between these 28 member states are significant, ranging from member states where quality expertise centres are available and those where some but not all necessary treatment is available. In Malta and

---

387. National contribution (sociological report) on the Russian Federation, p. 35.
388. Stonewall, "Prescription for Change. Lesbian and Women's Health Check", 2008, p. 14.
389. European Court of Human Rights, *Kiyutin v. Russia*, Application No. 2700/10, judgment of 10 March 2011, paragraph 74.
390. European Court of Human Rights, *van Kück v. Germany*, Application No. 35968/97, judgment of 12 June 2003, paragraph 82.
391. European Court of Human Rights, *L. v. Lithuania*, Application No. 27527/03, judgment of 11 September 2007, paragraph 59.

Ireland, for example, hormonal treatment is available, but no surgery. In yet other member states services are only available in one city.

In 13 member states (Albania, Andorra, Armenia, Azerbaijan, Bosnia and Herzegovina, Croatia, Liechtenstein, Lithuania, Luxembourg, Moldova, Monaco, Montenegro and San Marino) no facilities needed for gender reassignment treatments were identified. Transgender persons from these 13 countries wishing to undergo gender reassignment would then have to go abroad (they are explicitly advised to do so in some member states). For the remaining six member states information on availability of health facilities is unclear.

A person who wants to access gender reassignment treatment must usually meet a strict and unified "one size fits all" list of requirements. Such requirements may be based on legislation or regulations, though often this is rather a matter of custom and practice. Generally requirements include medical and psychological assessments of the applicant and/or the diagnosis of gender dysphoria or gender identity disorder (following the WHO classification). Yet other member states require applicants to undergo a "real-life experience" (RLE) by living in the preferred gender for a specified length of time, which varies by state. Doctors may assess the "success" of such RLE on the basis of the person's clothing taste and gender-normative behaviour. According to transgender persons, they have to perform in a highly stereotypical way, often going to the extremes in their preferred gender to fit the eligibility criteria. Other requirements include the risk of suicide of the client, absence of "homosexual inclinations", or vague concepts such as "no serious flaws in the ability for social adaptation".[392] Concerns have also been raised by transgender persons in relation to medical professionals who have large decision-making powers over their access to treatment.

Financial obstacles to accessing gender reassignment treatment

The European Court of Human Rights has required states to provide insurance to cover expenses for "medically necessary" treatment, which gender reassignment surgery is a part of.[393] However, research for this report shows that access to health care insurance is highly problematic in at least 16 countries (Albania, Andorra, Armenia, Azerbaijan, Bosnia and Herzegovina, Bulgaria, Georgia, Lithuania, Moldova, Montenegro, Poland, Romania, the Russian Federation, Serbia, Slovakia and Turkey). In these countries transgender persons claim that they must bear the financial burden of medically necessary health care themselves.

---

392. National contribution (legal report) on Ukraine, p. 32.
393. European Court of Human Rights, *van Kück v. Germany*, Application No. 35968/97, judgment of 12 June 2003, paragraphs 47, 73 and 82 and *L. v. Lithuania*, Application No. 27527/03, judgment of 11 September 2007, paragraphs 59 and 74.

In the remaining 31 member states, research for this report shows that there is partial or full reimbursement.[394] In Germany, Portugal, Sweden and Italy public health insurance covers most if not all expenses related to a person's gender reassignment treatment. In Greece, Iceland and Ireland, payment by public health insurance for treatment abroad has been reported, though not confirmed as a general rule. In San Marino, since gender reassignment facilities are not available in the country, transgender persons may have the costs of surgeries performed abroad reimbursed by the national health fund. Hungary's health insurance cover for gender reassignment treatment is 10% of the total costs. In the Netherlands, not all surgery is covered, and some surgery is covered only partially. Malta covers only hormone treatment. Norway covers costs for some but not all transgender persons, depending on the particular diagnosis of the person. In Switzerland private health insurance companies have in the past refused transgender people. In the judgment *Schlumpf v. Switzerland* the European Court of Human Rights found that the refusal of the insurance company to cover the costs of the applicant's gender reassignment surgery due to non-compliance with the requirement to complete two years of observation in order to ascertain the existence of "true transsexualism" was in violation of Article 8.[395] In the UK around 86% of transgender respondents claimed that they were refused state funding for surgery and more than 80% claimed they were refused funding for hormone treatment. Over half of transgender respondents said they had funded their own treatment.[396] Coverage of public health insurance is unclear in the countries not mentioned above.

6.3. Education

The right to education includes the right to receive information about sexual orientation and gender identity that is objective and knowledge-based. International standards take the view that impartial information can overcome prejudice and save people from inflicting or suffering violence. The UN Special Rapporteur on the Right to Education[397] views sex education as an important way of counteracting discrimination. The UN Committee on the Rights of the Child has recommended that states include sexual education in the curricula of primary and secondary schools,[398] which may

---

394. For a full overview, see the (FRA) national contributions (sociological and legal reports) on the mentioned countries.
395. European Court of Human Rights, *Schlumpf v. Switzerland*, Application No. 29002/06, judgment of 8 January 2009, paragraphs 115-16.
396. Whittle S., Turner L., Combs R., Rhodes S., "Transgender EuroStudy: Legal Survey and Focus on the Transgender Experience of Health Care", Brussels, 2008, p. 57.
397. Report of the United Nations Special Rapporteur on the Right to Education, A/65/162. 23 July 2010, paragraph 60.
398. Committee on the Rights of the Child, Concluding Observations: Antigua and Barbuda CRC/C/15/Add.247, paragraph 54; Committee on the Rights of the Child, Concluding Observations: Trinidad and Tobago, CRC/C/TTO/CO, paragraph 54.

also imply that laws that prevent young people educating themselves about their sexual orientation conflict with the Convention.[399]

The European Committee of Social Rights set an important standard in 2009 when it found that Croatia had breached the non-discrimination provisions of the European Social Charter by issuing teaching materials that were "biased, discriminatory and degrading, especially in the way they describe people whose sexual orientation is different from heterosexual".[400] The Croatian Ministry of Education later withdrew the biology textbook in question.

A 2010 resolution and recommendation of the Parliamentary Assembly as well as a Committee of Ministers recommendation include references to the right to education.[401] The Committee of Ministers pointed out that the right to education should be enjoyed without discrimination on grounds of sexual orientation or gender identity. This includes, among others, "safeguarding the right of children and young people to education in a safe environment, free from violence, bullying, social exclusion or other forms of discriminatory and degrading treatment related to sexual orientation or gender identity". The Committee of Ministers also stresses that "objective information with respect to sexual orientation and gender identity" must be provided, "for instance in school curricula and educational materials".[402]

Heteronormativity in education and teaching materials

There is a range of educational systems in Council of Europe member states. Some are determined centrally by government and others more autonomously by schools. Overall there seems to be little teaching material of good quality on LGBT issues.

In a significant number of member states, including Albania, Armenia, Azerbaijan, Belgium, Bosnia and Herzegovina, Bulgaria, Croatia, Denmark, Hungary, Ireland, Italy, Lithuania, Malta, Moldova, Montenegro, Poland, the Russian Federation, Serbia, Slovakia, Slovenia, "the former Yugoslav Republic of Macedonia" and Turkey, NGOs report that schools do not provide any information about homosexuality or if so only biased, incorrect information. Such schoolbooks and teaching materials tend to present incorrect information not reflecting the WHO de-classification of homosexuality. In Moldova, for instance, according to NGO reports, at the Medical University

---

399. Concluding observations: United Kingdom of Great Britain and Northern Ireland, CRC/C/15/Add.188, 9 October 2002, Adolescent health, paragraph 43.
400. *International Centre for the Legal Protection of Human Rights (INTERIGHTS) v. Croatia* – Collective Complaint No. 45/2007, decision of 30 March 2009, paragraphs 60-61.
401. Recommendation 1915 (2010) of the Parliamentary Assembly on discrimination on the basis of sexual orientation and gender identity; Resolution 1728 (2010) of the Parliamentary Assembly on discrimination on the basis of sexual orientation and gender identity; Committee of Ministers Recommendation CM/Rec(2010)5 on measures to combat discrimination on grounds of sexual orientation or gender identity, adopted on 31 March 2010, paragraphs 31-32.
402. Committee of Ministers Recommendation CM/Rec(2010)5 on measures to combat discrimination on grounds of sexual orientation or gender identity, adopted on 31 March 2010, paragraphs 31 and 32.

homosexuality is taught as a disease from text books written when it was still criminalised.[403] In "the former Yugoslav Republic of Macedonia" a book on "Pedagogy" intended for use in secondary schools includes a chapter on "Negative Aspects of Sexual Life" that describes gay and lesbian persons as "psychotic and highly neurotic" people participating in a "degenerated sexual life".[404] In Croatia the textbook *With Christ to Life* refers to religious dogmas describing homosexuality as "intrinsically disordered" and "contrary to the natural law".[405] In an academic thesis in 2004, a sociologist from the Russian Federation argued that academic discourse often presents homosexuality as a curable disease and a pathology.[406]

Even though in 2006 Spain introduced a law on "Education for Citizenship and Human Rights" with a view to recognising "emotional-sexual diversity",[407] an analysis of textbooks by NGOs[408] shows that only some publishing houses comply with the law's minimum standards. Surveys in Malta,[409] Slovenia[410] and Sweden[411] also point to heteronormative approaches in schools. Norway is one of the few member states to provide objective information about transgenderism in the state school curriculum. Research in Norway, however, suggests that, despite the good intentions, teachers commonly depict gay men and lesbians as "the other", something different and problematic, while heterosexuality is "normal" and "natural".[412] In the Netherlands, research shows that 50% of school textbooks pay attention to homosexuality and bisexuality, but they are silent on transgenderism.[413] The Equality and Human Rights Commission (EHRC) in the United Kingdom has studied the ways educational materials and schools ignore people who are transgender.[414]

---

403. National contribution (sociological report) on Moldova, p. 15.
404. Coalition for Protection and Promotion of Sexual and Health Rights, "Annual Report on sexual and health rights of marginalised communities", Skopje, 2009, p. 54.
405. Peri J., Vuica M. and Vuleti D., *With Christ to Life*, Kršćanska Sadašnjost, Zagreb, 2008, p. 16.
406. National contribution (sociological report) on the Russian Federation, p. 31.
407. FRA national contribution (legal report) on Spain, p. 54.
408. Federación Estatal de Lesbianas, Gays, Transexuales y Bisexuales, La diversidad afectivo-sexual y familiar en los manuales de "Educación para la Ciudadanía y los Derechos Humanos", Un estudio de los manuales de Educación para la Ciudadanía, 2008.
409. FRA national contribution (sociological report) on Malta, p. 10.
410. FRA national contribution (sociological report) on Slovenia, p. 7; Kuhar R. and Švab A., "Homophobia and Violence against Gays and Lesbians in Slovenia", *Revija za Sociologiju*, Vol. XXXIX, No. 4, 2008, pp. 267-81.
411. Reimers E., "Always somewhere else: heteronormativity in Swedish teacher training", in Martinsson L., Reimers E., Reingarde J. and Lundgren A. S. (eds), *Norms at Work. Challenging Homophobia and Heteronormativity*. TRACE: The Transnational Cooperation for Equality, 2006, pp. 59-61.
412. Røthing Å., "Gode intensjoner, problematiske konsekvenser. Undervisnig om homofili på ungdomsskolen", *Norsk Pædagogisk Tidsskrift*, vol. 91: 485-97, 2007; Røthing, Å., "Homonegativisme og homofobi i klasserommet: marginaliserte maskuliniteter, disiplinerende jenter og rådville lærere", *Tidsskrift for ungdomsforskning*, vol. 7(1): 27-51, 2007.
413. Korte B., Leurink A., Lodeweges J. and Ridderink M., *Homoseksualiteit in leermiddelen*, Nationaal InformatieCentrum Leermiddelen, SLO, Enschede, November 2001.
414. EHRC, "Provision of Goods, Facilities and Services to Trans People: Guidance for Public Authorities in Meeting Your Equality Duties and Human Rights Obligations", 2010, p. 39.

Absence of information at all stages of the curriculum helps maintain the invisibility of LGBT persons and it helps to maintain the absence of discussing sexual orientation and gender identity issues according to studies carried out in Hungary and Slovenia.[415] It should be stressed that this is often at an age that many may find out that they are LGB or T.

In some member states some good initiatives have been taken to counterbalance this trend. A national action plan in Norway targeted schools at both primary and secondary level and provided guidance for teachers and new teaching materials. These added an LGBT dimension to subjects in the mainstream curriculum.[416] The national study curriculum set by the Estonian Ministry of Education and Science provides a basis for discussions on LGB issues.[417] In Belgium, in 2007, public authorities subsidised a website and brochure on "gender diversity and transgender" for pupils of 14-18 years.[418] With older school students in mind, the Slovenia Peace Institute issued a CD-ROM in 2003 to help teachers discuss sexual orientation during classes.[419]

Homophobic and transphobic bullying and discrimination in educational settings

According to studies carried out across member states[420] and supported by some government research, LGBT students suffer from bullying from both peers and teachers. In a United Kingdom study among transgender persons it was found that some 64% of transgender men and 44% of transgender women reported experiencing harassment or bullying by their peers and sometimes by their teachers.[421] In Serbia, 21% of students surveyed admitted they had verbally attacked or threatened someone they thought was gay or "feminised", while 13% said they had actually helped beat them up. Some 60% of respondents held that violence against homosexual persons was always justified.[422] Research conducted by an NGO in the United Kingdom[423] found that homophobic language is widespread in schools. Some 90% of secondary

---

415. Takács J., Mocsonaki L., Tóth T. P., "Social Exclusion of Lesbian, Gay, Bisexual, and Transgender (LGBT) People in Hungary", Institute of Sociology, Hungarian Academy of Sciences, 2008; Kuhar R. and Švab A, "Homophobia and Violence against Gays and Lesbians in Slovenia", *Revija za Sociologiju*, Vol. XXXIX, No. 4, 2008, p. 271.
416. Norwegian Ministry of Children and Equality, "The Norwegian Government's action plan: Improving quality of life among lesbians, gays, bisexuals and trans persons, 2009-2012", 2008, pp. 19-20.
417. FRA national contribution (legal report) on Estonia. p. 33.
418. FRA national contribution (sociological report) on Belgium, p. 7.
419. European Union Agency for Fundamental Rights, "Homophobia and Discrimination on Grounds of Sexual Orientation and Gender Identity in the European Union Member States: Part II – The Social Situation", 2009, p. 78.
420. Takács J., "Social Exclusion of young lesbian, gay, bisexual and transgender (LGBT) people in Europe", ILGA-Europe and IGLYO, 2006. Also research in Albania, Bosnia and Herzegovina, Belgium, Germany, Hungary, Malta, Montenegro, the Netherlands, Norway, Ireland, Serbia, Slovenia, Turkey, Ukraine and the United Kingdom, and by ILGA-Europe.
421. Whittle S., Turner L., Al-Alami M., "Engendered Penalties: Transgender and Transsexual People's Experiences of Inequality and Discrimination", Wetherby: The Equalities Review, 2007, p. 17.
422. CARE International and International Center for Research on Women, Young Men Initiative for Prevention of Gender-Based Violence in Western Balkans, "Baseline Research Technical Brief – Country Report. Serbia", 2009, p. 8.
423. Stonewall UK, "Homophobic Bullying in Britain's Schools – The Teachers' Report", 2009.

schoolteachers said that pupils in their schools are bullied, harassed or called names for being – or for being perceived to be – homosexual. Half of the teachers who indicated that they are aware of homophobic bullying in school pointed out that the overwhelming majority of incidents are never officially reported or dealt with.

Some national human rights structures and NGOs have found that the management and staff of schools do too little to address bullying. In some other member states, such as in Ireland, a joint campaign of NGOs and the equality body have been set up, resulting in posters to all secondary schools with the message "Homophobic bullying is not acceptable in our schools".[424] However, even when anti-bullying policies are in place, they may provide inadequate protection or be insufficiently implemented. A United Kingdom study found that out of 300 schools observed, 82% were aware of verbal homophobia and 26% of physical homophobic bullying, even though almost all of these schools had anti-bullying policies in place.[425] Research in 2009 from the United Kingdom reported that a higher percentage of transgender persons experience bullying at school (75%) than lesbian, gay and bisexual persons (25%).[426]

Teachers who are gay, lesbian, bisexual or transgender can also suffer discrimination and harassment from their colleagues, students or their employer as such. In Romania the Ministries of Education and Health jointly introduced psychological testing for teachers in 2003 and forbade gay and lesbian persons to teach. Although the regulation was repealed, it was replaced in 2006 by another joint order, listing homosexuality among grounds for exclusion.[427] In some member states, including in the Netherlands and Lithuania, discussions have taken place regarding the equal treatment laws in these countries and the extent to which schools based on religion or belief may or may not be able to lawfully refuse to employ a gay or lesbian teacher (Netherlands) or limit educational awareness-raising activities on LGBT issues (Lithuania).[428] Cases against discrimination in education on grounds of sexual orientation or gender identity have been brought to national courts or equality bodies in Bulgaria, Croatia, Romania, Russia,[429] Turkey, Greece,[430] Italy[431] and Sweden.[432]

---

424. European Union Agency for Fundamental Human Rights, "Homophobia and Discrimination on Grounds of Sexual Orientation and Gender Identity in the European Union Member States: Part II – The Social Situation", 2009, p. 71.
425. Averill, S., "How can young people be empowered to achieve justice when they experience homophobic crime?", 2004, p. 20.
426. ECHR, "Provision of Goods, Facilities and Services to Trans People: Guidance for Public Authorities in Meeting Your Equality Duties and Human Rights Obligations", 2010, p. 40.
427. Romanian Ministry of Education and Research, Ministry of Health and the National Health Insurance Authority, Order No. 4840/IR 38342/2796/2005 on mandatory health check of school personnel.
428. European Union Agency for Fundamental Rights, "Homophobia, Transphobia and Discrimination on Grounds of Sexual Orientation and Gender Identity: 2010 Update – Comparative Legal Analysis", 2010, pp. 25-26.
429. National contribution (legal report) on the Russian Federation. pp. 45-46.
430. FRA national contribution (sociological report) on Greece, p. 8.
431. FRA national contribution (legal report) on Italy, p. 20.
432. HomO, Dossier No. 620-2006. Decision, 3 August 2007.

The negative consequences of bullying may be enormous. NGOs and studies in several member states point to the negative impact that bullying has on the school performance and well-being of LGBT students generally. Lesbian, gay, bisexual or transgender adolescents may not seek support from their families and/or community because they have not yet "come out" with their sexual orientation or gender identity, or because they had previously been rejected for doing so. Several studies show that a homophobic or transphobic environment at school may lead to higher drop-out rates of LGBT young persons from secondary school. These young people are also more likely to contemplate self-harm and engage in high-risk behaviour.[433] A study in the Russian Federation made similar findings.[434] Stress and social isolation are most acute for young people who become aware of their homosexuality during their years at school. Homophobia and bullying in school may damage the academic work of LGBT pupils and destroy their self-image and confidence. Studies moreover suggest that bullying has a negative impact on the health of LGBT persons[435] but the social stigma surrounding LGBT issues has delayed concerted public health research in member states.

School boards have a duty to provide a safe setting in which LGBT students and teachers are protected from bullying. Some good practice can be reported from the Netherlands, where an NGO coalition has developed a practical standard for managing a school that is safer for LGBT persons;[436] in the same country a handbook on student counselling includes a chapter on the needs of LGBT students.[437]

6.4. Employment

Work is essential both for personal development and for social and economic independence.[438] In financial terms, it implies the right to be able to ensure an adequate standard of living for oneself and one's dependants. The right to work is enshrined in Article 6 of the ICESCR[439] and Article 8 of the ICCPR.[440] There is an obligation for states to guarantee that the right to work can be exercised without discrimination of any kind.[441] In its General Comment No. 20, the UN

---

433. Jenett, M., "Stand up for us: Challenging homophobia in schools", Yorkshire, Crown Copyright, 2004, p. 10; IGLYO and ILGA-Europe, Written contribution to Schools for the 21st Century Commission Staff Working Paper (SEC (2007) 1009), December 2007.
434. Moscow Helsinki Group, "Situation of Lesbians, Gays, Bisexuals and Transgenders in the Russian Federation", Moscow, 2009, pp. 29-30.
435. For example, National Institute for Working Life. "Arbetsvillkor och utsatthet", Sweden, 2003; Jenett M., "Stand up for us – Challenging homophobia in schools", Department for Education and Skills, London, 2004, p. 8.
436. Schouten M. and Dankmeijer P., "Een roze draad in veiligheid op school", February 2008.
437. Dankmeijer P., "Homo- en transseksuele aandachtspunten in de leerlingenbegeleiding", in Toolkit Leerlingenbegeleiding, Kluwer, 2006.
438. UN Committee on Economic, Social and Cultural Rights, General Comment No. 18, 24 November 2005, Article 6, paragraph 4. See also General Comments Nos. 14, 15 and 20.
439. International Covenant on Economic, Social and Cultural Rights.
440. International Covenant on Civil and Political Rights.
441. Cf. UN Committee of Economic, Social and Cultural Rights, General Comment No. 18 of 24 November 2005, Article 6, paragraph 19.

Committee on Economic, Social and Cultural Rights lists sexual orientation and gender identity among prohibited grounds for discrimination. It recognises that "persons who are transgender, transsexual or intersex often face serious human rights violations such as harassment in schools or in the work place".[442]

The revised European Social Charter guarantees social and economic rights including the right to work[443] and the principle of non-discrimination applies to all rights set out in it. The Committee of Ministers Recommendation CM/Rec(2010)5 explicitly puts sexual orientation and gender identity among prohibited grounds for discrimination in the employment sphere. A specific provision covers effective protection of the privacy of transgender persons in relation to employment applications and disclosure of their gender identity history.[444]

The European Union Employment Equality Directive prohibits discrimination on grounds of sexual orientation in the private and the public sectors, not only in the place of employment, but also in procedures governing access to work, and in labour-related organisations. In 2009, the European Commission reviewed the Directive's[445] application in European Union member states to find that three member states had infringed the Employment Equality Directive's provisions against discrimination on the ground of sexual orientation (Poland,[446] the United Kingdom[447] and the Netherlands[448]). "Sex" discrimination in employment is currently the legal basis of European Union legislation to combat employment discrimination on the ground of gender reassignment. One of the employment cases before the Court of Justice of the European Union on discrimination on the grounds of gender identity produced a landmark judgment. In 1996 it found that dismissal of a transsexual person for reasons related to gender reassignment was precluded under the 1976 Equal Treatment Directive on prohibition of discrimination on the ground of "sex".[449]

In total, 38 member states regard sexual orientation as a prohibited ground for discrimination either in comprehensive non-discrimination

---

442. UN Committee on Economic, Social and Cultural Rights, General Comment No. 20 on non-discrimination, paragraph 32.
443. The European Social Charter, adopted in 1961 (ETS No. 35) and revised in 1996 (ETS No. 163).
444. Committee of Ministers Recommendation CM/Rec(2010)5 on measures to combat discrimination on grounds of sexual orientation or gender identity, adopted on 31 March 2010, paragraphs 29-30.
445. European Union Directive 2000/78/EC establishing a general framework for equal treatment in employment and occupation, Articles 7 and 10.
446. Reasoned Opinion sent on 29 January 2010 concerning the prohibition of discrimination on all grounds set out in the Directive (including sexual orientation) which is not provided for in regulations on access to certain professions according to the European Commission.
447. Reasoned Opinion sent on 23 November 2009 concerning the possibility of justifying discrimination on grounds of sexual orientation in case of employment by religious institutions which is considered too wide by the European Commission.
448. Reasoned Opinion sent on 1 February 2008 concerning the exceptions provided for legal relations within religious communities and employment by religious institutions which are considered to be too wide, also making it possible to discriminate unduly for example on grounds of sexual orientation.
449. Court of Justice of the European Union, C-13/94, *P. v. S. and Cornwall County Council*, judgment of 30 April 1996, paragraph 20.

legislation, or in employment-specific (sectoral) legislation. Even though this is an overwhelming majority of Council of Europe member states, the 2007 Eurobarometer survey showed that only 30% of European Union citizens were aware of laws prohibiting discrimination on grounds of sexual orientation in the labour market.[450]

Regarding gender identity, the situation is more complex. Nine member states have included gender identity explicitly in comprehensive non-discrimination legislation. At least 11 member states treat discrimination on grounds of gender identity or gender reassignment as a form of sex or gender discrimination in comprehensive non-discrimination legislation. In the remaining 27 member states the situation regarding coverage of transgender persons under non-discrimination legislation is unclear. These 27 member states include European Union member states which should as a minimum recognise, in the field of employment, discrimination of a person who intends to undergo or has undergone gender reassignment as a form of sex or gender discrimination.[451]

Discrimination and harassment against LGBT persons in the work place

LGB employees may experience the denial of benefits provided to heterosexual staff and their spouses such as parental leave; health care insurance for employees and their families; educational and leisure facilities for employees and their families; bereavement leave, or leave to care for a sick partner and survivor's benefit in occupational pension schemes. Discrimination against transgender persons may occur when they are not addressed by the correct name and/or pronoun or when they are denied time off work for gender reassignment therapy. In states where men and women retire at different ages, transgender women may be forced to wait for a state pension until they reach male retirement age.

Employees who are "out" at work, or suspected of being lesbian, gay, bisexual, or transgender, can experience indirect discrimination by employers, colleagues or clients which can include sexually explicit remarks intended to embarrass or ridicule. For example, according to the National Institute for Working Life[452] some 30% of lesbian and bisexual women in Sweden say that demeaning comments at work are the norm.

The scale of discrimination against LGBT persons in the work place is hard to estimate. Very few member states compile statistics on discrimination in the employment sector, and statistics that exist are generally not disaggregated in a meaningful way. Research for this report revealed that between 2005 and 2010 a handful of employment discrimination cases came to court or equality bodies in at least 21 Council of Europe member states (Austria,

---

450. European Commission, Special Eurobarometer 263, "Discrimination in the European Union", 2007, p. 30.
451. See chapter 2.3 for a full overview of national non-discrimination legislation.
452. National Institute for Working Life. Arbetsvillkor och utsatthet, Sweden, 2003, p. 73, also quoted in European Union Agency for Fundamental Rights, "Homophobia and Discrimination on Grounds of Sexual Orientation and Gender Identity in the European Union Member States: Part II – The Social Situation", 2009, p. 68.

Belgium, Cyprus, the Czech Republic, Denmark, Estonia, France, Germany, Hungary, Latvia, Lithuania, Italy, the Netherlands, Norway, Poland, Romania, the Russian Federation, Spain, Sweden, Turkey and the United Kingdom).[453] In addition to these data, surveys reveal that significant numbers of LGBT persons claim to have been discriminated against at work; however, those incidents are not formally reported. These surveys include 52% of LGBT workers in the United Kingdom surveyed by a trade union; 39% of lesbian and gay workers surveyed in Denmark;[454] over a third of respondents in Hungary;[455] 56% of transgender employees surveyed in Spain.[456]

Examples of claims of discrimination and harassment cases identified for this report include a Croatian civil servant who was given an office in the basement and told that a "faggot should die in the basement with rats". Supervisors reportedly did not respond to his memo, and he was reluctant to bring a charge against the ministry.[457] A transgender woman in Moldova claimed to have been dismissed from her post as a high-school teacher during her hormone therapy, despite requests from her students' parents to let her stay.[458]

Under-reporting may be endemic. Some equality bodies and NGOs think this is because LGBT persons risk more than most other people if they complain.[459] By irrevocably "coming out" with a complaint in the workplace, they fear, like other complainants, being victimised and dismissed. Unlike other complainants, however, they fear they will never be able to conceal their sexual orientation or gender identity in the future and so become permanently unemployed, especially if they live in a small town where the social control is strong. It is fear of dismissal and long-term unemployment that prompts many LGBT persons to adopt a protective silence.[460]

A report by ILGA-Europe suggests that homophobic and transphobic attitudes often prevail in the workplace because employers hesitate to tackle what is often considered a difficult subject to address. The report says that "many people are simply not aware that their colleagues may experience their daily work lives in a fundamentally different manner. ... Some argue that sexual

---

453. (FRA) national contributions (legal reports) contain annexes with descriptions on such cases identified in the member states. See also European Union Agency for Fundamental Rights, "Homophobia and Discrimination on Grounds of Sexual Orientation and Gender Identity in the European Union Member States: Part II – The Social Situation", 2009, p. 64.
454. European Union Agency for Fundamental Rights, "Homophobia and Discrimination on Grounds of Sexual Orientation and Gender Identity in the European Union Member States: Part II – The Social Situation", 2009, p. 68.
455. Takács J., Mocsonaki L. and Tóth T. P., A leszbikus, meleg, biszexuális és transznem (LMBT) emberek társadalmi kirekesztettsége Magyarországon (Social Exclusion of LGBT People in Hungary), MTA SZKI, Budapest, 2007.
456. Esteva, I. et al. "Social Inequalities: Demographic Characteristics of Patients Treated at the First Gender Identity Disorder Unit in Spain", 2001.
457. National contribution (legal report) on Croatia, p. 31.
458. National contribution (sociological report) on Moldova, p.16.
459. For example Walsh J., Conlon C., Fitzpatrick B. and Hansson U., Enabling Gay, Lesbian and Bisexual Individuals to Access their Rights under Equality Law, Equality Authority and Equality Commission for Northern Ireland, 2007, p. 47.
460. Moscow Helsinki Group, "Situation of Lesbians, Gays, Bisexuals and Transgenders in the Russian Federation", 2009, p. 45.

orientation is a private matter, best confined to the bedroom and that it has no relevance to the workplace".[461] In employment sectors where traditional notions of masculinity and femininity prevail, it may be a serious problem for people who challenge gender norms to find employment.

The impact on victims and strategies to end discrimination

LGB persons tend to conceal their sexual orientation in the workplace. The Eurobarometer survey found that 68% of European Union citizens think that it is difficult for a homosexual person to state his/her sexual orientation in the workplace.[462] An investigation in Sweden found that 50% of LGB respondents were not "out" at work and 40% avoided socialising with colleagues for fear of having to share such private details with colleagues.[463] This pattern was also identified in empirical studies in Albania,[464] Croatia,[465] Finland,[466] Germany,[467] Norway,[468] Poland,[469] the Russian Federation[470], Slovakia,[471] and in an ILGA-Europe report.[472]

Transgender persons who decide to undergo gender reassignment treatment could face the opposite problem, especially during the period of gender reassignment treatment. Surveys suggest that up to 77% of transgender employees do not tell their employers about their gender identity and 50% of them find this stressful. They may find themselves pushed to the margins of the job market and out of formal employment, which in some Council of Europe member states results in transgender women working in the sex industry.

LGB persons may be more productive at work if they do not need to conceal their sexual orientation. Some firms in member states have used this argument and argued for the "business-case for diversity", which resulted in

---

461. Quinn S. and Paradis E., "Going beyond the law: promoting equality in employment", ILGA-Europe, Brussels, 2007, pp. 10-11.
462. European Commission, Special Eurobarometer 263, "Discrimination in the European Union", 2007, p. 13.
463. National Institute for Working Life. Arbetsvillkor och utsatthet, Sweden, 2003, pp. 123-24.
464. GISH, "Survey Research with the LGBT community in Albania", Tirana, 2006.
465. Lesbian Group Kontra, "Violence Against Lesbians, Gays and Bisexuals in Croatia: research report", Zagreb, 2006, p. 39.
466. Lehtonen J. and Mustola K. (eds), *"Straight People Don't Tell, Do They?": Negotiating the Boundaries of Sexuality and Gender at Work*, Ministry of Labour, Helsinki, 2004, pp. 4-5.
467. Frohn D. (ed.), "'Out im Office?!' Sexuelle Identität, (Anti-)Diskriminierung und Diversity am Arbeitsplatz", Schwules Netzwerk NRWe.V., Cologne, 2007, p. 7.
468. Moseng B. U., "Lesbiske og homofile arbeidstakere – en pilotundersøkelse", NOVA, Oslo, 2005.
469. Abramowicz M. (ed.), "The Situation of Bisexual and Homosexual Persons in Poland: 2005 and 2006 Report", Campaign Against Homophobia and Lambda Warsaw Association, Warsaw, 2007.
470. Moscow Helsinki Group, "Discrimination based on Sexual Orientation and Gender Identity in the Russian Federation", Moscow, 2007.
471. Daucikova A., Jojárt P. and Siposova M., "Report on Discrimination of Lesbians, Gay Men and Bisexuals in Slovakia", Documentation and Information Centre, Bratislava, 2002.
472. Quinn S. and Paradis E., "Going Beyond the Law: Promoting Equality in Employment", ILGA-Europe, Brussels, 2007, p. 24.

LGBT employee networks being established and partner benefits to both LGB and heterosexual workers given.[473] In France, 150 large employers have agreed to check their employment practices for compliance with a diversity charter devised by the High Authority for Equality and the Elimination of Discrimination (HALDE).[474] The NGO Stonewall in the United Kingdom has developed a 25-question online survey to help employers assess how well they perform on equality issues. An International Gay and Lesbian Chamber of Commerce has been set up, and has developed an International Business Equality Index based on Stonewall's survey.

Some good practice can be reported from member states. A lesbian NGO, ŠKUC, in Slovenia has tried to change public attitudes to LGBT persons through TV adverts that show LGBT Slovenian celebrities at their work places. The same organisation, in co-operation with the Slovenian Ministry of Labour, Family and Social Affairs, published two manuals on "Measures against employment discrimination" to be used by trade unions and employers.[475]

Some 55% of European Union citizens thought in a Eurobarometer survey in 2009 that not enough efforts were made to combat employment discrimination based on grounds of sexual orientation.[476] Trade unions play in this regard a crucial role in preventing discrimination on grounds of sexual orientation and gender identity. Some national unions in Poland and Italy have appointed staff to focus on LGBT issues. In 2006, a Polish trade union defended gay and lesbian teachers against homophobic comments by Polish officials.[477] In 2007 the European Trade Union Confederation (ETUC) adopted targets for raising LGBT awareness and tackling prejudice among its members[478] and in 2008 it held the first Europe-wide trade union conference on LGBT rights.

Non-discrimination legislation is the first step towards combating discrimination in the workplace against LGBT persons, but it needs to be effectively implemented. Public sector employers can give a strong lead in this area and tools exist for them to facilitate the process. The United Kingdom introduced a public sector gender equality duty, which requires all public authorities and their contractors to include transgenderism among eight prohibited grounds of discrimination and to promote equality of transgender women and men.

---

473. Quinn S. and Paradis E., "Going Beyond the Law: Promoting Equality in Employment", ILGA-Europe, Brussels, 2007, p. 26.
474. FRA national contribution (legal report) on France, p. 15.
475. Greif T., "Ukrepi proti diskriminaciji v zaposlovanju za sindikat", ŠKUC, Ljubljana 2006; Greif T., "Ukrepi proti diskriminaciji v zaposlovanju za delodajalce", ŠKUC, Ljubljana, 2006.
476. European Commission, Special Eurobarometer 317, "Discrimination in the EU", 2009, p. 33.
477. European Commission, "Trade Union Practices on Anti-Discrimination and Diversity", pp. 34-36.
478. European Trade Union Confederation, "The Seville Manifesto", adopted by the XIth ETUC Congress, Seville, 21-24 May 2007.

Conclusions

This report provides a socio-legal overview of the human rights situation of LGBT persons in the 47 Council of Europe member states. It identifies serious flaws as well as positive developments in the protection from discrimination on grounds of sexual orientation and gender identity in several thematic fields. The report also looks beyond the legislative frameworks and clearly demonstrates that LGBT persons continue to be subjected to homophobia and transphobia in their everyday lives. Further efforts by member states are needed to pursue legislative reforms and social change to enable LGBT persons to fully enjoy universally recognised human rights.

Attitudes and perceptions

Despite the fact that criminalisation and medicalisation of homosexuality belong to the past in Europe, attitudes towards gay, lesbian and bisexual persons are often still characterised by outdated and incorrect information on what constitutes someone's sexual orientation. Transgender persons continue to face a particularly medicalised and prejudiced environment. Homophobic and transphobic attitudes have been identified in all member states, though attitudes vary significantly among and within the 47 member states of the Council of Europe. There is an urgent need to counterbalance such attitudes and deeply rooted prejudices by disseminating unbiased and factual information on sexual orientation and gender identity in the media, in schools and society at large.

Invisibility of LGBT persons and the absence of sexual orientation and gender identity in relevant human rights debates have turned out to be recurring themes during the data collection for this report. At the most basic level, many LGBT persons remain invisible in everyday life out of fear of negative reactions at school, at work, in their neighbourhood or in their family. They fear that being "out" will lead to harassment, rejection, physical violence and discrimination. Many LGBT individuals conceal their sexual orientation or gender identity and adjust to the heteronormativity present in society. Several member states have introduced programmes promoting education and dialogue with a view to challenging negative attitudes towards LGBT persons. Such initiatives need to be consistently followed across Europe to counterbalance negative stereotypes.

Legal standards and their implementation

A large majority of member states have adopted legislation to prohibit and eliminate discrimination against persons because of their sexual orientation. Transgender persons, however, receive less clear protection in existing non-discrimination legislation in most member states. When they are included in the scope of protection, it is often not explicit or the protection does not go beyond a limited concept of gender identity, which seriously diminishes its impact. There is an urgent need for member states to remedy this situation by introducing "gender identity" as an explicit ground of discrimination in non-discrimination legislation.

The extent of discrimination against LGBT persons on grounds of their sexual orientation and gender identity is hard to determine with precision due to the non-availability of official data in most member states. This sharply contrasts with data on discrimination provided by NGOs. There is a need for member states to review the accessibility to and effective implementation of non-discrimination legislation in view of this incongruence between officially available data and the information provided by civil society. National structures for promoting equality have a key role to play in combating discrimination based on sexual orientation and gender identity and making their complaint mechanisms accessible to LGBT persons. However, many of them lack an explicit mandate to address discrimination on grounds of sexual orientation and the situation is even worse regarding the ground of gender identity.

Comprehensive equal treatment legislation should be accompanied with appropriate policy measures for its implementation. A handful of member states of the Council of Europe have initiated national policies to address discrimination of LGBT persons in the employment sector and bullying of young LGBT persons at school or in other sectors. Other member states could draw inspiration from such initiatives.

Protection: violence and asylum

LGBT persons run a serious risk of becoming victims of hate crimes or hate-motivated incidents. Such violence, inspired by the perpetrators' deeply felt hatred and rejection of the real or perceived sexual orientation or gender identity of the victim, is rarely specifically addressed in member states' legislation. Under-reporting of such violence is a problem as victims do not trust law-enforcement agencies, which may lack proper training to investigate effectively hate-motivated crimes, speech and incidents. Even if incidents or crimes are reported, there is ample evidence that the bias motivation is not usually reflected in official statistics as homophobic and transphobic motives are not recognised by most member states in relevant legislation. Discriminatory and inflammatory language against LGBT persons, including by politicians and religious figures, compounds the problem and paves the way for a climate where hate-motivated incidents occur without a strong public condemnation, but are rather condoned. Member states should step up efforts to combat hatred against LGBT persons.

In the area of asylum claims, a majority of member states recognise that sexual orientation can be a ground of persecution in asylum claims under the notion of "membership of a particular social group". However, the recognition that gender identity can also be a ground for people to flee their countries is only recognised in a handful of states. Member states should draw inspiration from relevant UNHCR guidelines concerning the international protection of LGBT asylum seekers.

Participation: freedoms of assembly, expression and association

Too often, violent and discriminatory reactions occur when LGBT persons join together to form associations, express their views or demonstrate in public. While in most member states the freedoms of association, expression, and assembly of LGBT persons are respected, in a few countries bans or administrative impediments have been imposed on peaceful LGBT demonstrations in recent years. In some instances, the police have failed to protect peaceful demonstrators from violent assaults. When such bans and impediments happen, LGBT organisations often have to apply to courts in order to overturn decisions by authorities. The same phenomena can be seen when LGBT associations try to register their organisations: some bans have again been overturned by courts. There is no justification for member states to impose bans on LGBT organisations and peaceful assemblies as the European Court of Human Rights has set up clear standards in this regard. The same goes for attempts to criminalise "propaganda of homosexuality" as it violates the freedom of expression.

Privacy: gender recognition and family life

Transgender persons face significant problems in their efforts to have their preferred gender legally recognised. The absence of relevant legislation as well as cumbersome and unclear procedures in most member states contribute to a failure by many member states to recognise the preferred gender of transgender persons. Twenty-nine member states require gender reassignment surgery whereas 15 member states require the transgender person to be unmarried, which entails mandatory divorce if the person is already married. There is an urgent need for member states to review and adapt their legislation in light of the Recommendation of the Committee of Ministers as well as recent legislative reform in a few member states.

Same-sex couples who wish to legally seal their relationships face significant challenges in most Council of Europe member states. Even though family law is to a great extent a matter of national competence, under European human rights law it is becoming increasingly difficult to justify differential treatment between same-sex couples and different-sex couples when accessing rights and benefits if the only difference is the sexual orientation of the partners involved. The European Court of Human Rights has recognised that same-sex partners enjoy "family life" with reference to the European Convention and come under its protection in this area as well.

Access to health care, education and employment

LGBT persons encounter a wide range of problems in accessing health care. Limited knowledge and awareness among health professionals of the health problems of LGBT persons and the denial of treatment are only some of the identified obstacles. Moreover, contrary to international medical classifications, medical professionals in some member states may still be taught that homosexuality is an illness. Transgender persons face particular problems in accessing health care. In 13 member states the infrastructure suitable for gender reassignment treatment is non-existent or insufficient. Transgender persons have no other choice than to go abroad to receive treatment. Furthermore, a person wanting to access gender reassignment treatment must usually meet a strict "one size fits all" list of requirements, which include the diagnosis of gender dysphoria. A fundamental shift towards a human rights approach for transgender persons is necessary to address the excessively medicalised practices of today.

Bullying at schools is present in the lives of LGBT persons from a very early stage in practically all member states. Only in very few member states are policies in place to combat bullying and harassment of LGBT students, teachers, and staff. Consequently, schools are not experienced as a safe environment for LGBT persons. Textbooks may transmit information that homosexuality is an illness; these do not contribute to a healthy development of young LGBT persons. Member states should do more to prevent bullying and provide objective information in schools.

LGBT persons are affected by discrimination in the employment sector. Even though the majority of national non-discrimination legislations include sexual orientation as one of the discrimination grounds in the employment sphere, gender identity is usually not included even if it may be partially covered by the ground of gender or sex. Not only do transgender persons face particular problems when accessing the labour market, they also encounter issues concerning privacy and the disclosure of personally sensitive data related to their gender identity history. The concept of reasonable accommodation should be further developed in this context to improve the access of transgender persons to employment. Some trade unions and employers have set up policies and practices in order to foster diversity in the workplace encouraging the full inclusion of LGBT staff. Such initiatives need to be supported by member states.

Data collection, research and monitoring

The general lack of official data on discrimination on grounds of sexual orientation and gender identity as well as homophobia and transphobia is a significant obstacle to remedial measures. There is a need for member states to collect data on these issues. Without such data there can be no solid basis for informed decision making and monitoring, which is crucial for addressing the many human rights challenges identified in this report. When privacy concerns are properly addressed, setting up data-collection mechanisms can be the start of developing and implementing policies combating discrimination and intolerance on grounds of sexual orientation and gender identity. This can of course only be successful when there is the political will to recognise that problems exist and that discrimination, transphobia and homophobia need to be combated – and that progress has to be monitored. Some member states have experience in this field and could share their good practices, which could form the basis for a development establishing a set of clear and reliable indicators and benchmarks.

Wider outlook

An important premise for drafting this report has been to offer a tool for dialogue with the authorities of the 47 member states of the Council of Europe. In this regard it can be considered a baseline study for further action in both legislative and policy fields. The Committee of Ministers Recommendation from 2010 has already provided the political impetus to take concrete steps to develop and implement effective policies for preventing sexual orientation and gender identity discrimination in all member states of the Council of Europe.

National and international monitoring is needed to measure progress in all fields covered by this report. Within member states, national structures for promoting equality have an important role to play in monitoring. Civil society organisations representing LGBT persons should be able to participate in this process. The Council of Europe and its monitoring mechanisms have added value to offer. The Council of Europe should also provide assistance to member states in implementing the European and international standards in this field.

Moreover, as this report has demonstrated, the standards set by the 47 member states of the Council of Europe bear a direct influence on the protection afforded to LGBT persons from countries where they face persecution, repression or even the death penalty for being LGBT. There is a need to take stock of this fact and bring it to the attention of other fora for the wider promotion of human rights. Converging efforts by the Council of Europe, the European Union, the OSCE and the UN to implement human rights without discrimination are essential for ensuring the full enjoyment of universal rights by LGBT persons everywhere.

Appendix: Terms and concepts

This report uses a number of terms and concepts which are defined and clarified below in order to facilitate the full understanding of the report. The definitions are not considered exhaustive. While referring to the list, one should bear in mind that some of the terms may have slightly different meanings in various contexts and in different languages.

Discrimination is legally defined as unjustified, unequal treatment:

- **Direct discrimination** occurs when for a reason related to one or more prohibited grounds (for example, sexual orientation and gender identity) a person or group of persons is treated less favourably than another person or another group of persons is, has been, or would be treated in a comparable situation; or when, for a reason related to one or more prohibited grounds, a person or group of persons is subjected to a detriment.[479]

- **Indirect discrimination** occurs when a provision, criterion or practice would put persons having a status or a characteristic associated with one or more prohibited grounds (including sexual orientation and gender identity) at a particular disadvantage compared with other persons, unless that provision, criterion or practice is objectively justified by a legitimate aim, and the means of achieving that aim are appropriate and necessary.[480]

- **Experienced discrimination**, also called subjective discrimination, is the experience of being discriminated against. Experienced discrimination does not necessarily entail discrimination in the legal sense.[481]

Gender identity refers to a person's deeply felt individual experience of gender, which may or may not correspond with the sex assigned at birth, and includes the personal sense of the body and other expressions of gender (that is, "gender expression") such as dress, speech and mannerisms.[482] The sex of a person is usually assigned at birth and becomes a social and legal fact from there on. However, some people experience problems identifying with the sex assigned at birth – these persons are referred to as "transgender" persons. Gender identity is not the same as sexual orientation, and transgender persons may identify as heterosexual, bisexual or homosexual.[483]

---

479. The Equal Rights Trust, *Declaration of Principles on Equality*, London, 2008, pp. 6-7.
480. Ibid.
481. Olli E. and Olsen B. K. (eds), "Towards Common Measures for Discrimination: Exploring possibilities for combining existing data for measuring ethnic discrimination", Danish Institute for Human Rights, 2005.
482. Definition based on the Yogyakarta Principles on the Application of International Human Rights Law in relation to Sexual Orientation and Gender Identity, 2006.
483. Commissioner for Human Rights, "Human Rights and Gender Identity", Issue Paper, Strasbourg, 2009, pp. 5-6.

Gender marker is a gendered designator on, for example, an identity document (passports). The most obvious gender markers are designations such as male/female or Mr/Mrs/Ms/Miss. They can also be professional titles or personal pronouns, or coded numbers, such as social security numbers and tax numbers which may use certain combinations for men and for women (for example, even/uneven numbers). Gender markers are often embedded in ID cards or personal certificates such as passports, birth certificates, school diplomas, and employers' reference letters.

Gender reassignment treatment refers to different medical and non-medical treatments which some transgender persons may wish to undergo. However, such treatments may also often be required for the legal recognition of one's preferred gender, including hormonal treatment, sex or gender reassignment surgery (such as facial surgery, chest/breast surgery, different kinds of genital surgery and hysterectomy), sterilisation (leading to infertility). Some of these treatments are considered and experienced as invasive for the body integrity of the persons.

Harassment constitutes discrimination when unwanted conduct related to any prohibited ground (including sexual orientation and gender identity) takes place with the purpose or effect of violating the dignity of a person or creating an intimidating, hostile, degrading, humiliating or offensive environment.[484] Harassment can consist of a single incident or several incidents over a period of time. Harassment can take many forms, such as threats, intimidation or verbal abuse, unwelcome remarks or jokes about sexual orientation or gender identity.

Hate crime towards LGBT persons refers to criminal acts with a bias motive. Hate crimes include intimidation, threats, property damage, assault, murder or any other criminal offence where the victim, premises or target of the offence are selected because of their real or perceived connection, attachment, affiliation, support or membership of an LGBT group.[485] There should be a reasonable suspicion that the motive of the perpetrator is the sexual orientation or gender identity of the victim.[486]

Hate-motivated incident is used in this chapter to encompass incidents, acts or manifestations of intolerance committed with a bias motive that may not reach the threshold of hate crimes, due to insufficient proof in a court of law for the criminal offence or bias motivation, or because the act itself may not have been a criminal offence under national legislation.[487]

---

484. The Equal Rights Trust, *Declaration of Principles on Equality*, London, 2008, p. 7.
485. OSCE/ODIHR, "Hate Crimes in the OSCE Region – Incidents and Responses. Annual Report for 2009", Warsaw, 2010, p. 13.
486. See Committee of Ministers Recommendation CM/Rec(2010)5 on measures to combat discrimination on grounds of sexual orientation or gender identity, adopted on 31 March 2010.
487. OSCE/ODIHR, "Hate Crimes in the OSCE Region – Incidents and Responses. Annual Report for 2009", Warsaw, 2010, p. 13; Committee of Ministers Recommendation on measures to combat discrimination on grounds of sexual orientation or gender identity, CM/Rec(2010)5, adopted on 31 March 2010.

Hate speech against LGBT people refers to public expressions which spread, incite, promote or justify hatred, discrimination or hostility[488] towards LGBT people – for example, statements made by political and religious leaders or other opinion leaders circulated by the press or the Internet which aim to incite hatred.

Heteronormativity can be defined as the institutions, structures of understanding and practical orientations that make heterosexuality seem coherent, natural and privileged. It involves the assumption that everyone is heterosexual, and that heterosexuality is the ideal and superior to homosexuality or bisexuality. Heteronormativity also includes the privileging of normative expressions of gender – what is required or imposed on individuals in order for them to be perceived or accepted as "a real man" or "a real woman" as the only available categories.[489]

Homophobia is defined as an irrational fear of, and aversion to, homosexuality and to lesbian, gay, bisexual and transgender persons based on prejudice.[490] **Transphobia** refers to a similar phenomenon, but specifically to the fear of, and aversion to, transgender persons or gender non-conformity. Manifestations of homophobia and transphobia include discrimination, criminalisation, marginalisation, social exclusion and violence on grounds of sexual orientation or gender identity.[491]

Intersex people are persons who are born with chromosomical, hormonal levels or genital characteristics which do not correspond to the given standard of "male" or "female" categories as for sexual or reproductive anatomy. This word has replaced the term "hermaphrodite", which was extensively used by medical practitioners during the 18th and 19th centuries. Intersexuality may take different forms and cover a wide range of conditions.[492]

LGBT people or **LGBT persons** is an umbrella term used to encompass lesbian, gay, bisexual, and transgender persons. It is a heterogeneous group that is often bundled together under the LGBT heading in social and political arenas. Sometimes LGBT is extended to include intersex and queer persons (LGBTIQ).

Multiple discrimination describes discrimination that takes place on the basis of several grounds operating separately.[493] Another term often used in

---

488. Based on the definition in Committee of Ministers Recommendation No. R(97)20 on "hate speech", adopted on 30 October 1997.
489. Based on Warner M., "Introduction: Fear of a Queer Planet", Social Text, 9 (4 [29]), 1991, pp. 3–17; Rosenberg T., Queerfeministisk Agenda, Arena, Stockholm, 2002; RFSL, *Open Up Your Workplace: Challenging Homophobia and Heteronormativity*, 2007.
490. European Parliament resolution on homophobia in Europe (P6_TA(2006)0018 (PE 368.248)).
491. Committee of Ministers Recommendation CM/Rec(2010)5 on measures to combat discrimination on grounds of sexual orientation or gender identity, adopted 31 March 2010.
492. World Health Organization, "Genetic components of Sex and Gender". See also Federal Anti-Discrimination Agency, Benachteiligung von Trans Personen, insbesondere im Arbeitsleben, Berlin, 2010, p. 11.
493. European Commission, Tackling Multiple Discrimination. Practices, Policies and Laws, 2007.

this regard is **intersectional discrimination**, which refers to a situation where several grounds operate and interact with each other at the same time in such a way that they are inseparable.[494]

Queer is a term laden with various meanings and a long history, but currently often denotes persons who do not wish to be identified with reference to traditional notions of gender and sexual orientation and eschew heterosexual, heteronormative and gender-binary categorisations. It is also a theory, which offers a critical perspective into heteronormativity.

Sexual orientation is understood to refer to each person's capacity for profound emotional, affectional and sexual attraction to, and intimate and sexual relations with, individuals of a different gender (heterosexual) or the same gender (homosexual, lesbian, gay) or more than one gender (bisexual).[495]

Transgender persons include persons who have a gender identity which is different from the gender assigned to them at birth and those people who wish to portray their gender identity in a different way from the gender assigned at birth. It includes those people who feel they have to, prefer to, or choose to, whether by clothing, accessories, mannerisms, speech patterns, cosmetics or body modification, present themselves differently from the expectations of the gender role assigned to them at birth. This includes, among many others, persons who do not identify with the labels "male" or "female", transsexuals, transvestites and cross-dressers.[496] A transgender man is a person who was assigned "female" at birth but has a gender identity which is "male" or within a masculine gender identity spectrum. A transgender woman is a person who was assigned "male" at birth but has a gender identity which is female or within a feminine gender identity spectrum. Analogous labels for sexual orientation of transgender people are used according to their gender identity rather than the gender assigned to them at birth. A heterosexual transgender man, for example, is a transgender man who is attracted to female partners. A lesbian transgender woman is attracted to female partners. The word **transgenderism** refers to the fact of possessing a transgender identity or expression.

Transsexual refers to a person who has a gender identity which does not correspond to the sex assigned at birth and consequently feels a profound need to permanently correct that sex and to modify bodily appearance or function by undergoing gender reassignment treatment.

Transvestite (cross-dresser) describes a person who regularly, although part-time, wears clothes mostly associated with the opposite gender to her or his birth gender.

---

494. Ibid.
495. Yogyakarta Principles on the Application of International Human Rights Law in relation to Sexual Orientation and Gender Identity, 2008.
496. Definition based on Commissioner for Human Rights, "Human Rights and Gender Identity". Issue Paper, Strasbourg, 2009.

Sales agents for publications of the Council of Europe

BELGIUM/BELGIQUE
La Librairie Européenne -
The European Bookshop
Rue de l'Orme, 1
BE-1040 BRUXELLES
Tel.: +32 (0)2 231 04 35
Fax: +32 (0)2 735 08 60
E-mail: order@libeurop.be
http://www.libeurop.be

Jean De Lannoy/DL Services
Avenue du Roi 202 Koningslaan
BE-1190 BRUXELLES
Tel.: +32 (0)2 538 43 08
Fax: +32 (0)2 538 08 41
E-mail: jean.de.lannoy@dl-servi.com
http://www.jean-de-lannoy.be

**BOSNIA AND HERZEGOVINA/
BOSNIE-HERZÉGOVINE**
Robert's Plus d.o.o.
Marka Maruliça 2/V
BA-71000, SARAJEVO
Tel.: + 387 33 640 818
Fax: + 387 33 640 818
E-mail: robertsplus@bih.net.ba

CANADA
Renouf Publishing Co. Ltd.
1-5369 Canotek Road
CA-OTTAWA, Ontario K1J 9J3
Tel.: +1 613 745 2665
Fax: +1 613 745 7660
Toll-Free Tel.: (866) 767-6766
E-mail: order.dept@renoufbooks.com
http://www.renoufbooks.com

CROATIA/CROATIE
Robert's Plus d.o.o.
Marasoviçeva 67
HR-21000, SPLIT
Tel.: + 385 21 315 800, 801, 802, 803
Fax: + 385 21 315 804
E-mail: robertsplus@robertsplus.hr

**CZECH REPUBLIC/
RÉPUBLIQUE TCHÈQUE**
Suweco CZ, s.r.o.
Klecakova 347
CZ-180 21 PRAHA 9
Tel.: +420 2 424 59 204
Fax: +420 2 848 21 646
E-mail: import@suweco.cz
http://www.suweco.cz

DENMARK/DANEMARK
GAD
Vimmelskaftet 32
DK-1161 KØBENHAVN K
Tel.: +45 77 66 60 00
Fax: +45 77 66 60 01
E-mail: gad@gad.dk
http://www.gad.dk

FINLAND/FINLANDE
Akateeminen Kirjakauppa
PO Box 128
Keskuskatu 1
FI-00100 HELSINKI
Tel.: +358 (0)9 121 4430
Fax: +358 (0)9 121 4242
E-mail: akatilaus@akateeminen.com
http://www.akateeminen.com

FRANCE
La Documentation française
(diffusion/distribution France entière)
124, rue Henri Barbusse
FR-93308 AUBERVILLIERS CEDEX
Tél.: +33 (0)1 40 15 70 00
Fax: +33 (0)1 40 15 68 00
E-mail: commande@ladocumentationfrancaise.fr
http://www.ladocumentationfrancaise.fr

Librairie Kléber
1 rue des Francs Bourgeois
FR-67000 STRASBOURG
Tel.: +33 (0)3 88 15 78 88
Fax: +33 (0)3 88 15 78 80
E-mail: librairie-kleber@coe.int
http://www.librairie-kleber.com

**GERMANY/ALLEMAGNE
AUSTRIA/AUTRICHE**
UNO Verlag GmbH
August-Bebel-Allee 6
DE-53175 BONN
Tel.: +49 (0)228 94 90 20
Fax: +49 (0)228 94 90 222
E-mail: bestellung@uno-verlag.de
http://www.uno-verlag.de

GREECE/GRÈCE
Librairie Kauffmann s.a.
Stadiou 28
GR-105 64 ATHINAI
Tel.: +30 210 32 55 321
Fax.: +30 210 32 30 320
E-mail: ord@otenet.gr
http://www.kauffmann.gr

HUNGARY/HONGRIE
Euro Info Service
Pannónia u. 58.
PF. 1039
HU-1136 BUDAPEST
Tel.: +36 1 329 2170
Fax: +36 1 349 2053
E-mail: euroinfo@euroinfo.hu
http://www.euroinfo.hu

ITALY/ITALIE
Licosa SpA
Via Duca di Calabria, 1/1
IT-50125 FIRENZE
Tel.: +39 0556 483215
Fax: +39 0556 41257
E-mail: licosa@licosa.com
http://www.licosa.com

MEXICO/MEXIQUE
Mundi-Prensa México, S.A. De C.V.
Río Pánuco, 141 Delegacíon Cuauhtémoc
MX-06500 MÉXICO, D.F.
Tel.: +52 (01)55 55 33 56 58
Fax: +52 (01)55 55 14 67 99
E-mail: mundiprensa@mundiprensa.com.mx
http://www.mundiprensa.com.mx

NETHERLANDS/PAYS-BAS
Roodveldt Import BV
Nieuwe Hemweg 50
NE-1013 CX AMSTERDAM
Tel.: + 31 20 622 8035
Fax.: + 31 20 625 5493
Website: www.publidis.org
Email: orders@publidis.org

NORWAY/NORVÈGE
Akademika
Postboks 84 Blindern
NO-0314 OSLO
Tel.: +47 2 218 8100
Fax: +47 2 218 8103
E-mail: support@akademika.no
http://www.akademika.no

POLAND/POLOGNE
Ars Polona JSC
25 Obroncow Street
PL-03-933 WARSZAWA
Tel.: +48 (0)22 509 86 00
Fax: +48 (0)22 509 86 10
E-mail: arspolona@arspolona.com.pl
http://www.arspolona.com.pl

PORTUGAL
Livraria Portugal
(Dias & Andrade, Lda.)
Rua do Carmo, 70
PT-1200-094 LISBOA
Tel.: +351 21 347 42 82 / 85
Fax: +351 21 347 02 64
E-mail: info@livrariaportugal.pt
http://www.livrariaportugal.pt

**RUSSIAN FEDERATION/
FÉDÉRATION DE RUSSIE**
Ves Mir
17b, Butlerova ul.
RU-101000 MOSCOW
Tel.: +7 495 739 0971
Fax: +7 495 739 0971
E-mail: orders@vesmirbooks.ru
http://www.vesmirbooks.ru

SPAIN/ESPAGNE
Mundi-Prensa Libros, s.a.
Castelló, 37
ES-28001 MADRID
Tel.: +34 914 36 37 00
Fax: +34 915 75 39 98
E-mail: libreria@mundiprensa.es
http://www.mundiprensa.com

SWITZERLAND/SUISSE
Planetis Sàrl
16 chemin des pins
CH-1273 ARZIER
Tel.: +41 22 366 51 77
Fax: +41 22 366 51 78
E-mail: info@planetis.ch

UNITED KINGDOM/ROYAUME-UNI
The Stationery Office Ltd
PO Box 29
GB-NORWICH NR3 1GN
Tel.: +44 (0)870 600 5522
Fax: +44 (0)870 600 5533
E-mail: book.enquiries@tso.co.uk
http://www.tsoshop.co.uk

**UNITED STATES and CANADA/
ÉTATS-UNIS et CANADA**
Manhattan Publishing Company
468 Albany Post Road
US-CROTON-ON-HUDSON, NY 10520
Tel.: +1 914 271 5194
Fax: +1 914 271 5856
E-mail: Info@manhattanpublishing.com
http://www.manhattanpublishing.com

Council of Europe Publishing/Editions du Conseil de l'Europe
FR-67075 STRASBOURG Cedex
Tel.: +33 (0)3 88 41 25 81 – Fax: +33 (0)3 88 41 39 10 – E-mail: publishing@coe.int – Website: http://book.coe.int